LAL BAHADUR SHASTRI

LAL BAHADUR SHASTRI
POLITICS AND BEYOND

~Sandeep Shastri~

RUPA

Published by
Rupa Publications India Pvt. Ltd 2019
7/16, Ansari Road, Daryaganj
New Delhi 110002

Sales Centres:

Allahabad Bengaluru Chennai
Hyderabad Jaipur Kathmandu
Kolkata Mumbai

ISBN: 978-93-5333-660-8

First impression 2019

10 9 8 7 6 5 4 3 2 1

The moral right of the author has been asserted.

Dedicated to
My wife, Shailaja,
for being my anchor of support, with the steadfastness of her
convictions, the strength of her character, the firmness of her
resolve and her unflinching faith in my capabilities.

CONTENTS

INTRODUCTION

A Simple Life

It is now over half a century since Lal Bahadur Shastri, the second prime minister (PM) of Independent India passed away. Those of us who grew up in India and were 'socialized' in the last fifty years would have come across fleeting references to Shastri in our history textbooks as the one who led the country against Pakistan during the 1965 war. Those who delve a little deeper into history would remember him as the one who coined the slogan '*Jai Jawan, Jai Kisan*' (Hail the Soldier, Hail the Farmer), which, to date, remains the most powerful slogan of self-reliance. Beyond this, chroniclers of history have not given Shastri the space he deserves or the attention he merits as one of those leaders who shaped the course of developments in the country in the first two decades after Independence. Possibly because he succeeded Jawaharlal Nehru, who led the country for seventeen long years, the spotlight of attention is often on the first PM of India rather than his immediate successor. This could also be because of the distinctly different personalities of the two men. Shastri was a diminutive figure, almost self-effacing, who preferred to remain in the background. He rarely spoke and when he did, it was in a measured tone. On the other hand, Nehru was a towering personality in every sense of the term. He was a charismatic leader who was often the centre of attention and was known for his oratorical skills in both English and Hindi.

Shastri was India's PM for a mere nineteen months. In that year and a half, he faced many a political challenge and dealt with each one of them most effectively. However, his tenure is considered by many to be too short to have had a lasting impact. A deeper analysis of Shastri's time as the PM provides clear proof of the success of his style and the impact of his leadership. If he had had the chance to lead the country a little longer, he could well have shaped the course of Independent India's history in a different way. Yet, one realizes that history is not necessarily about ifs and buts! It must also be conceded that the near-domination of the Nehru-Gandhi family in the leadership of the Congress party in the seventy years after Independence has provided very little scope and space to leaders like Shastri, Pamulaparthi Venkata (P.V.) Narasimha Rao or Dr Manmohan Singh to secure their legitimate share of recognition in shaping and moulding the course of Independent India's politics. It is in this context, that the current work attempts an assessment of Shastri's political career from the time of his entry into the freedom movement till his untimely death as the sitting PM.

◆

Having opted for the social sciences right from school, I was fascinated with the leadership of Shastri as it always caught my attention. Researching for this book allowed me to delve deeper into his life and times. As one reads more and more about Shastri and hears about him from those who had been his associates, one gets to understand his unique personality and inimitable style of leadership. As generations grow up in 21st-century India, it may be useful to recall incidents, anecdotes, episodes, experiments and individuals who contributed to the making of Independent India. While the focus has always been on the Father of the Nation, Mahatma Gandhi, and the first PM, Nehru, very little is said and known about Shastri. He chose a path that was different, was quietly assertive and patiently non-compromising. This makes the cataloguing of his life and achievements so very fascinating. One would be doing a disservice to the history of post-Independence India if the rightful place and stature are not accorded to leaders like Shastri. This work is a humble and honest effort in that direction.

I was not even six years old when Shastri passed away. Having lived in Delhi at that point of time, I have vague memories of sitting down in front of the radio with my parents and elder brother to listen to PM Shastri speak to the nation. The radio then was an important mode of communication in the absence of the television. I have vivid memories of the days of the war with Pakistan when the sirens at night would signal people to switch off the lights in their homes. One could hardly see anything through the windows as they would be covered with black paper to prevent any light from escaping. I still remember my father reminding me in hushed tones of what PM Shastri had said in his last broadcast and I felt proud as a five-year-old that I was faithfully following his instructions to remain calm. One realized in one's own way that the country was facing danger and was passing through a crisis. My parents kept assuring my brother and me that India was safe under Shastri's leadership.

A leading politician of those days who belonged to the

Praja Socialist Party (PSP), Hari Vishnu Kamath, was a family friend. Whenever my father was posted in Delhi, Kamath mama (as we called him) used to come home at least once a week for dinner and used to regale us with stories and anecdotes. Even though Shastri and he were from rival political parties, he had the greatest respect and highest regard for Shastri. Kamath mama's eyes used to sparkle whenever he spoke of Shastri. He often mentioned that Shastri had friends from across the political spectrum. He used to frequently consult and take into confidence members from the Opposition, a practice that was abandoned by his successors. As a member of the Administrative Reforms Commission constituted during Shastri's time (he was the only member from the Opposition who was on the Commission), Kamath mama was all admiration for the long-term vision of Shastri in constituting a body to review the administrative system and suggest reforms accordingly. Kamath mama also often referred to Shastri's sincere efforts to tackle corruption and nepotism in the administration.

To take this narration forward, it may be useful to highlight the qualities that made Shastri and his leadership style unique, as well as the principles he stood for, which won him admiration and respect from all quarters. When the Congress party took the decision to choose, by consensus, Shastri to succeed Nehru as the PM, there were three important public statements that he made:

- The first was his acceptance speech made at the meeting of the Congress Parliamentary Party (CPP), when he was chosen as the leader. While accepting the leadership, Shastri assured his party that he would discharge his duties 'with utmost humility' but not hesitate to seek their help, cooperation and understanding. 'If you do it [cooperate], you will add to my strength and make my efforts fully successful,' he said.[1] Shastri gave expression to his core values when he said that he accepted the responsibility with humility. Given his consensus-building approach, he sought their cooperation and pleaded for their understanding. He emphasized that their support and understanding were key to his success. Clearly, an approach of inclusiveness was for him the pathway to achieving success. Many saw this humility as meekness, but in retrospect, it was his core strength and enhanced his acceptability.

• The second was at his first press conference soon after his selection, where he made a broader appeal to the citizens of the country to remain united in dealing with the challenges the country was facing. He said that the nation must stand as one and tackle problems as effectively and quickly as they can. While affirming that he had full faith in the citizens of the country, he said, 'Sometimes we—those who are called leaders—might have failed. They [the people] have not.'[2] These words were not a result of any rhetorical flourish but the deep and abiding faith in the innate goodness and wisdom of the common people.

• The third was his first radio address to the nation,

[1]With Utmost Humility—Text of Thanksgiving Speech of Shri Lal Bahadur Shastri, in the Central Hall of Parliament, 2 June 1964, Shri Lal Bahadur Shastri—*Abhinandan Granth* (A Souvenir) Edited by S.M. Shaffee, p. 125.
[2]Message to the Nation—On 2 June 1964, while meeting the press, Shri Lal Bahadur Shastri—*Abhinandan Granth* (A Souvenir) Edited by S.M. Shaffee, p. 123.

as the PM, where he was more philosophical and reiterated his faith in democracy and socialism.

In important ways, these three statements highlight the person he was, the values he stood for and the principles he believed in.

Earlier, at the Bhubaneswar session of the Congress, a few months before he took over as PM, he had piloted the resolution on democratic socialism as PM Nehru was unwell. He had vigorously defended the need to dovetail the principles of democracy and socialism. He gave expression to similar sentiments in his first address to the nation as PM. His unequivocal commitment to peace with other nations was outlined as part of his larger global vision. His focus on continuity with change was evident. Even as he referred to the crossroads of history, he was categorical in stating that the road he chose was clear and straight and involved a commitment to the ideals that guided the leadership of the past[3]:

> There comes a time in the life of every nation when it stands at the crossroads of history and must choose which way to go... Our way is straight and clear— the building up of a socialist democracy at home with freedom and prosperity for all, and the maintenance of world peace and friendship, with all nations abroad. To that straight road and these shining ideals we rededicate ourselves today.

---

[3]Prosperous India and World Without War—Fitting Memorials to Gandhiji and Jawaharlal. First Broadcast to the nation as Prime Minister by Shri Lal Bahadur Shastri, 11 June 1964, Shri Lal Bahadur Shastri—*Abhinandan Granth* (A Souvenir) Edited by S.M. Shaffee, p. 125.

NON-CONFRONTATIONIST LEADERSHIP STYLE

As Shastri began his tenure as India's PM, the key elements of his leadership style were evident in his initial pronouncements. His unshakeable faith in democracy and individual freedom was at the core of his beliefs. Ensuring the prosperity of all and the progress of the nation was a commitment he made to the people. He stretched out his hand of friendship to all nations of the world in general and India's neighbours in particular. He promised to tread the path of consultation and consensus, approached his responsibilities with humility and saluted the spirit of tolerance and self-restraint of the Indian people. These leadership traits, which were clearly on test during the nineteen months of Shastri's tenure as the PM, had been honed and built up during the four decades that preceded his rise to this top position.

Shastri's journey in politics was one of natural progression. It was a step-by-step movement forward, with every new recognition and responsibility being based on the skills acquired and accomplishments demonstrated in the past phase. He was a leader who rose from the grass roots and had the benefit and experience of working at multiple levels. His understanding of India's problems was born out of that active engagement, participation and interaction with the common people of India. He was a self-made man, with no family background in politics to provide him with a head start or name. His steady rise was verily the byproduct of his proven capacities, hard work and sincere efforts.

Leaders who went on to become his mentors recognized his potential, leveraged his skills and entrusted him with important responsibilities. Right from his school days, teachers were drawn to his organizational capacities and entrusted him with important tasks of coordination. During the freedom struggle, he was a key local organizer in the Non-cooperation Movement, Swadeshi campaign as well as the Quit India agitation. His dedicated work with the Servants of the People Society (SPS) saw his meteoric rise in the organization. Within the United Provinces[4], he was appointed to key positions in the Congress party. In the years prior to Independence, he had joined the government in the United Provinces as parliamentary secretary to the chief minister (CM) and rose to become a minister in the Cabinet in the first post-Independence government in the province.

When the Congress party was gearing itself to prepare for the first general elections of 1951–52, Shastri was brought to New Delhi to take charge as the general secretary (GS) of the party. In this role, he coordinated the selection of candidates both at the national and state levels, and monitored the key elements of the election campaign of the Congress party. After the Congress won a resounding majority in the 1952 polls, he joined the Union Council of Ministers. He remained in the Cabinet for the next fourteen years, handling important portfolios.

There were two brief phases when he stepped out of the government and was entrusted with party responsibilities. In 1956, he resigned on moral grounds as the railway minister after a major rail accident, to return to the Cabinet the very

---

[4]Until 25 January 1950, the province was referred to as United Provinces. Following Independence, the princely states of Rampur, Benaras and Tehri-Garhwal were merged into the United Provinces of what was British India. On 25 January 1950, the province was renamed 'Uttar Pradesh' (UP) and they came to be referred to as states rather than as provinces. In this book, the term 'United Provinces' is used for developments prior to 25 January 1950 and the term 'UP' is used after this period.

next year after the 1957 elections. His second resignation was in 1963 as part of the Kamaraj Plan (named after Kumaraswami Kamaraj, former CM of the erstwhile Madras Province and senior Congress leader), when a select number of senior ministers resigned to take on organizational responsibilities in the party. He was back in the Cabinet very soon, when PM Nehru fell ill and sought his presence in the Cabinet to carry on with some of the responsibilities of the PM. On Nehru's death, he was unanimously selected as the leader of the Congress Legislature Party and was sworn in as the PM. He remained in this position for a brief yet eventful and memorable tenure of nineteen months, until death snatched him away in 1966.

The above narration provides proof of what was earlier referred to as his steady climb up from the grass roots. He was involved with local politics and the government, and went on to state-level politics. He finally ascended to national politics, leading the country as PM. At each stage, the faith and confidence reposed in him were on account of him being able to balance his head and heart. It could also be argued that responsibilities and positions were entrusted to him and he personally neither pursued nor sought them. While his critics could argue that Shastri benefitted from having powerful mentors, it must be asserted that though he diligently followed instructions and was trusted for his loyalty, he had a mind of his own and would not hesitate to state a view that went contrary to what the leadership believed in. His greatest asset was his capacity to make a point with humility and sincerity. He was also known for thinking of all sections of people before arriving at decisions, which were based on consensus and consultation.

PERSONAL INTEGRITY ABOVE ALL ELSE

Right from his school days till the time he became the PM, Shastri stood out for the premium he placed on personal integrity. The subsequent chapters contain a range of examples from different phases of his life, wherein Shastri gave the highest degree of importance to personal integrity. He constantly reminded his family members of the need to maintain a clean image in public life and took immediate corrective action when any family member unwittingly transgressed the limits of personal probity. In his entire life, there was not even a whiff of a scandal involving his actions as a minister even though he drove policy initiatives in important ministries in the state and at the centre, such as home affairs, railways, transport, commerce and industry. Many political leaders who have held these portfolios have been trapped in the whirlpool of corruption, nepotism and misuse of their office. Yet during his career, Shastri steered a path that was consciously marked by transparency and steadfast adherence to principles. It is recorded that he purchased his first car when he became PM and that too after securing a loan. When he passed away, a part of the loan was still to be paid. His wife, Lalita Shastri, paid off the rest from the pension she received.

A linked dimension is that even when he was a minister, he assiduously avoided falling prey to the trappings of power. Once again, this narration is replete with examples of how despite being in a position of power, it did not allow Shastri to either lose touch with reality or compromise on the values he was committed to. Even as he occupied the highest office, he stayed away from many of the practices and behaviours that often, consciously or unconsciously, creep into the lifestyle and mannerisms associated with power and position. There was no expression of any arrogance associated with his holding prominent and distinguished positions both in the government and within the party. He retained his characteristic humility and down-to-earth approach. While many wondered whether this modesty was a front or put-on act to fend off criticism and disarm opponents, those who were associated with him saw a genuine and sincere attempt to be natural. Even those opposed to him politically would concede (some grudgingly) that it was difficult to criticize Shastri on his simplicity and modesty.

Shastri's lifestyle did not undergo any major change, regardless of whether he occupied a position in government or was out of it. His associates recall that when he resigned as the railway minister, he was found late one evening, sitting in the drawing room of his home with the lights switched off. On being asked, he mentioned that now that he did not hold any position in the government, he would need to pay for the family's maintenance from his own resources and, therefore, wished to reduce power consumption. There are also several anecdotes narrated in this study, wherein Shastri counsels his young children not to be enamoured by the privileges of power as they would need to learn to live life without these privileges also.

His dressing sense remained the same throughout his career. His clothes were simple and he was always neatly turned out. Many a time, Nehru encouraged him to dress more stylishly, but he remained his unpretentious self. On a visit to Srinagar during winter, Nehru gave Shastri his woollen overcoat as he knew that Shastri did not possess one. Once Shastri's sister bought him an expensive jacket and packed it in his bag when he was going on a tour, but it came back unused. The PM of the Union of Soviet Socialist Republics (USSR), Alexei Kosygin recalled an episode during the Tashkent Conference in 1966.

Given the cold weather in Tashkent, Kosygin gifted Shastri a warm overcoat for his use. A few days into the conference, Kosygin noticed that Shastri preferred to use the coat that he had brought from India. On enquiring whether he did not like the overcoat, Shastri replied that he gave the overcoat to a team member who had not brought sufficient warm clothing with him! Kosygin hailed Shastri as someone who practised communist principles more strongly than even the communists in USSR![5]

Free of any ideological trappings or rigidity, Shastri made himself acceptable to all streams of thought by the sincerity of his intentions and the commitment to his principles. A steadfast votary of Gandhian ideals, he never lost an opportunity to quote the Mahatma when the occasion or situation demanded. Often described as a 'Quintessential Gandhian', the Mahatma was the one who inspired him to enter the freedom struggle. The path that Gandhiji followed continued to be the inspiration for Shastri till his very last day. On the morning of the signing of the Tashkent Agreement, Shastri said to those around him that signing the accord was the one greatest tribute he could pay to the Mahatma. He went on to add that it would be a negation of the values that the Mahatma stood for if he did not work towards creating an environment to foster peace, harmony and non-violence.

An attempt has been made in this work to capture both his simple personality and style as well as the complexity of the diverse ways in which he resolved conflicts and differences of opinion, which ensured a convergence that satisfied opposing groups and interests. It is this legacy and contribution of Shastri that is most cherished.

---

[5]Choudary, P. & Shastri, A. (2015). *Lal Bahadur Shastri: Lessons in Leadership*, Delhi: Wisdom Village Publications, p. 154

1

UNDERSTANDING HIS POLITICS AND PRINCIPLES

The key to understanding an individual is to assess the principles that he upholds, the value systems that he follows and the legacy that he leaves behind. One's personality is often shaped by their life experiences and the learnings that they carry forward from critical milestones. Especially when people come to play a leadership role in public life and politics, the strength of their character, the influence of their personality and the power of their presence all go to shape their public image. History recalls human beings and their contributions not merely by chronicling their actions and achievements. It goes a step further and explores the traits and skills that contributed to their story. This chapter makes a similar attempt in the case of Lal Bahadur Shastri. It delves into the core ideals that defined the life and accomplishments of India's second PM. Leaders are often assessed in a context. That context gives meaning and provides a rationale to explain their attainments, assess their successes and situate their many life changes. This is imperative to be able to effectively relate to the niche that such leaders carve for themselves in history. One is not attempting here to merely catalogue Shastri's personality traits and his value system. The endeavour is to go a step further and delve a bit deeper. Understanding Shastri as an individual within the framework of his many life experiences will help to relate better to his principles and politics. That is the conscious effort in this narration.

The renowned businessman and philanthropist Ghanshyam Das Birla captured the essence of what attracted so many of those who had the privilege of interacting with Shastri. He said that Shastri is 'not a Leftist, but not Rightist either. He is a good, clean man.'[1] At times, even simple words can capture the essence of an individual! For people who met Shastri, he came across as a good man—in terms of his temperament, his people skills, and his simplicity and transparency. Those who were associated with him for longer and worked with him when he occupied public office are unanimous in their assertion of his commitment to the highest ethical standards. This is what Birla meant when he said that Shastri was a 'clean' man. This 'goodness' and 'cleanness' is reflected in much of what he said and did and, more critically, in the way he said what he said and did what he did.

It would also be useful to chronicle the reflections of two individuals who knew him from his younger days as a student. In the Diamond Anniversary issue of Kashi Vidyapeeth, the institution where Shastri completed his higher education, two of his contemporaries dwell at length on Shastri, the individual. Tribhuvan Narain Singh, who was his classmate, recalled, 'Shastri had the capacity to work ceaselessly without getting tired, he had no ill will towards those with whom he differed, and even those opposing him had an affection for him.'[2]

---

[1]Hangen, W. "After Nehru, Who?" *Champion of Peace: Tribute to Shastri* by Sudarshan K. Savara, New Delhi: Gyan Mandir, 1967, p. 37
[2]Singh, L.P. (1996). *Portrait of Lal Bahadur Shastri: A Quintessential Gandhian*. Ravi Dayal Publisher

LIMITLESS ENERGY

In the aforementioned statement, Singh highlights three characteristics that seemed second nature to Shastri: his energy levels, bearing no ill will towards people and being able to receive affection even from opponents. His limitless energy to work was his most prized asset. Those associated with Shastri were amazed at the long hours he devoted every day to work and the high energy levels he maintained even at the end of a long day packed with engagements. Visitors who came to his home or office always got an audience with him and left satisfied after having received a patient hearing. There were occasions when those who came had to leave without meeting him as their bus was due to depart. In one such instance, when Shastri came to know that the guests had left as they had to board a bus, he himself went to the bus stand, met the people there, saw them off and then returned home. As a minister, when he travelled to different cities, he often spent the night with his team at the airport, making sure that everyone had been provided for before having his meals himself.

His children and grandchildren used to be around him even as he completed his morning shave. He was also known for considering all sections of people before arriving at a resolution, which were based on consensus and consultation. Meals at home were occasions to exchange experiences with family members about the day's events. Even on his last day, after signing the Tashkent Agreement, Shastri remained awake till late into the night, seeking feedback from his core team and back home in India, to gauge popular responses to the accord. A major concern of the officers who worked with him was his punishing daily schedule, which he followed unmindful of his health. The officers who worked with him observed that he 'survives on a diet of long hours and hard work'. In spite of two heart attacks, Shastri had been back at work, spending very little time on rest and recuperation.

Right from his days as the parliamentary secretary to UP CM Govind Ballabh Pant, to the days when he became the PM, Shastri's schedule began early in the morning and went on till late into the night. He would never retire for the day until he had met his last visitor. He would personally see them off and make sure that they had transport arrangements for wherever they had to go. Associates recall that even at the end of the day after his last meeting, his energy levels remained as high as they were when he began the day.

PRIZED PEACEMAKER AND TEAM PLAYER

Shastri's classmate T.N. Singh had pointed out that Shastri bore no negative feelings towards those who differed with him. London-based *The Times*, commenting on Shastri's traits, had said, his 'large kind eyes suggest affection and sensibility'.[3] Writing in a similar vein, Canadian political scientist and professor Michael Brecher asserted that Shastri was a 'man virtually without political enemies'.[4] When Shastri resigned along with others as part of the Kamaraj Plan, he was the only one to be brought back to the ministry within a few months as Minister without Portfolio (MWP). Though there were a few murmurs on his reinduction, it was generally accepted that an unwell Nehru required the support of Shastri. Morarji Desai differed from Shastri on many occasions and

---

[3]*The Times*. (1964, June 14). [All quotes from *The Times* are from the microfilms in the Nehru Memorial Library (NML).]

[4]Brecher, M. (1966). *Succession in India: A Study in Decision-making.* Oxford University Press, p. 77

was his key rival when the question of choosing a successor to Nehru arose. Yet, they had the best of personal equations. When Shastri's mortal remains returned from Tashkent, Desai was among those present at the airport in Delhi to pay his respects. His interactions with his peers in the Parliament underscored the respect and admiration they had for him even though they differed on matters of policy and practice. During the two debates on the no-confidence motions (NCMs) against his government, the criticisms were largely linked to the government's style of functioning or ministers speaking in discordant voices. Even the few leaders from among the ranks of the Opposition, who took on Shastri directly, were extremely careful in the language that they used to criticize him. Shastri's response to the debate often disarmed the opponent, and he never lost his poise or capacity to remain polite. One of his associates in the Lok Sabha observed that when hurt, Shastri betrayed pain rather than anger, which only shamed the attacker.

During a debate in the Parliament, Vijaya Lakshmi Pandit referred to Shastri and his government as having become a 'prisoner of indecision'. Soon after the speech, she happened to meet Shastri and enquired whether there was anything remiss in her remarks. Shastri replied, '*Aapne jo theek samjhaa woh kaaha*' (You said what you thought was right). Commenting on that episode, Shastri's close aide Chandrika Prasad Srivastava says in his biography that Shastri had just faced a public onslaught on his credibility from an unexpected quarter, yet he had taken the incident with his usual equanimity.[5] Thus, it was difficult to name anyone who was an 'enemy' of Shastri, though

---

[5]Srivastava, C.P. (1995). *Lal Bahadur Shastri: A Life of Truth in Politics*. Oxford University Press, pp. 133–4.

many had serious differences with him on critical issues of policy and governance. His capacity to take everyone along was an important virtue.

In the same Diamond Anniversary issue of Kashi Vidyapeeth, another associate of Shastri's, Vishvanatha Sharma, recalls that Shastri 'never said anything even in jest, which could hurt'.[6] Someone who carefully chose his words and thought deeply before he uttered something, his true skill was the empathy he demonstrated in his interactions with people. In all the major crises he resolved, a key element was his 'choice of words' in one-to-one conversations. His sons, Anil and Sunil, in their writings, recall several examples of how he would get them around to his way of thinking through gentle persuasion and not by any use of authority, instruction or command. In later chapters we will talk about how Shastri would get people to take ownership for tasks he wanted them to do rather than merely assigning responsibilities. His favourite phrase, *'Aap hamaare saath chalenge?'* (Will you come along with me?), often persuaded people to take the initiative proactively.

There is an important and oft-quoted incident relating to a leading Congressman, Shankar Dayal Sharma, who later went on to become the president of India. When Shastri became PM, Sharma was a senior Congress leader in Madhya Pradesh. Sharma met Shastri and expressed a desire to move to national politics. Shastri's response was careful and measured. He told Sharma, 'Although you will be an asset to me in Delhi, who will be my man in Madhya Pradesh?' Sharma got his answer and continued to be involved in political activity in

---

[6]Singh, L.P. (1996). *Portrait of Lal Bahadur Shastri: A Quintessential Gandhian.* Ravi Dayal Publisher

Madhya Pradesh. Shastri's 'no' was presented in an extremely 'acceptable' manner.

This quality of never hurting anyone made Shastri a prized peacemaker as well as an exceptional team player. At school, he was the one who often reconciled differences between peers. During his stays in the SPS, a key skill he put to test was reconciling serious disputes in the villages, linked to caste, status and hierarchy. When he participated in the freedom movement and spent time in jail, he even settled differences between inmates, leaving no scope for the jail authorities to intervene. As Congress GS in 1952, he resolved a crisis among warring factions in the Congress and at the district and state level, and got them to work together in the first elections after Independence. When he joined the Union Cabinet, PM Nehru sought his support to try and iron out differences in policy positions with other Cabinet colleagues prior to a formal Cabinet meeting. His role as peacemaker was truly put to test during the Tashkent talks. The different rounds of discussions that he had with Ayub Khan of Pakistan and Kosygin of the Soviet Union were a testimony to his skills to seek peace between nations that shared a highly tensed relation.

Shastri's associates have remarked that there was nothing aggressive about him except his humility![7] While some have made the point that 'humility' could well have been a 'mask' of self-protection, those close to him would assert that this trait came naturally to him. L.P. Singh believes that Shastri's humility was a corollary to his deeply introspective nature, the spiritual influences in his life and his reflective approach

---

[7]Singh, L.P. (1996). *Portrait of Lal Bahadur Shastri: A Quintessential Gandhian*. Ravi Dayal Publisher.

to human relationships.[8] One could add to this list, the many experiences of life that also played a role in shaping this important virtue in Shastri. Irrespective of the position he occupied, he would always rise to greet visitors, offer them a seat and wish them goodbye with folded hands.

An important work that Shastri translated from English to Hindi while in jail, was the biography of the world-renowned scientist Marie Curie. What seemed to have appealed to Shastri about her was not merely her skills as a scientist, but also the moral and ethical values she upheld. Shastri writes about Curie's achievements: 'It is the finest tribute to any human endeavour that it should be untouched by pride and egoism despite success.'[9] In important ways, Shastri exhibited in himself the qualities he admired in Curie.

The American journalist Welles Hangen concurs and elaborates that Shastri's 'rare humility and genuine compassion set him apart. He has never succumbed to the disease of feeling superior which afflicts so many [educated] Indians.'[10] Hangen's reflections on the pride and arrogance, in those days, among Indians who had access to higher education, is in stark contrast to the behavioural traits that Shastri demonstrated. One has witnessed in contemporary times that access to power brings with it arrogance and haughtiness, which often distances the holder of power from both the people around them as well as the ground reality. The real test of a person's humility is not when they are out of power but when they are entrusted with it. One is often a witness today to the haughty attitude of not

---

[8]Singh, L.P. (1996). *Portrait of Lal Bahadur Shastri: A Quintessential Gandhian*. Ravi Dayal Publisher

[9]Verghese, B.G. "The Middle Way—Premier Designate Shastri." *A Study of Lal Bahadur Shastri*, B.S. Gujarati, Delhi: Sterling, 1965, p. 55

[10]Hangen, W. (1963). *After Nehru, Who?*. Harcourt, Brace & World

just those who wield power but those who surround them. To rephrase Lord Acton, the flavour of today seems to be power intoxicates and absolute power intoxicates absolutely. One notices this heady intoxication among political leaders within a very short span of their becoming ministers. The sea of difference in their attitude and approach is often patently visible when one compares their behaviour and disposition between the time they took their oath of office as ministers and five years down the line. Shastri was a shining example of humility even at the height of his power and privilege. His associates would endorse the fact that there was no visible change in his approach to people from the time he was minister for police and transport in the Cabinet of G.B. Pant in UP, till the time he went to Tashkent as PM to participate in a dialogue with Pakistan.

TIME FOR EVERYONE

C.P. Srivastava, who worked closely with Shastri for well over two decades, recalls two early encounters with him.[11] Srivastava first met Shastri soon after he joined the Indian Administrative Service and was posted as the city magistrate of Lucknow. He was advised by the district magistrate of Lucknow to call on Shastri, who was then the minister for home and transport, and seek his advice. Srivastava sought an appointment and was given one at 6 p.m. at Shastri's official residence. Srivastava arrived a few minutes before the scheduled time of the appointment and noticed that Shastri's official car was waiting at the entrance, with the rear door open. Shastri's personal assistant informed Srivastava that

---

[11]Srivastava, C.P. (1995). *Lal Bahadur Shastri: A Life of Truth in Politics.* Oxford University Press

since the home minister (HM) had been called for an urgent meeting with the CM, his appointment would be rescheduled.

Shastri soon appeared in the doorway and greeted a few guests present there. The personal assistant went up to him and pointing out to Srivastava, conveyed something. Immediately, Shastri moved towards Srivastava (who was standing some distance away) and greeted him with folded hands. Srivastava recalls that he was completely awed by a minister taking the initiative to greet a junior civil servant. Shastri requested Srivastava to join him inside in his drawing room. While Srivastava did suggest that the meeting could be rescheduled, Shastri insisted that the meeting be held. His initial queries related to whether Srivastava had been given a residence and had settled down.

During the brief conversation, the advice that Shastri gave remained with Srivastava as a guiding principle. Shastri told him that Lucknow needed a clean and efficient administration: 'There is also a need for constant vigilance about the law and order situation. The relations between the police and people must be based on mutual regard and respect.' He concluded by mentioning to Srivastava that the district magistrate was an extremely able and experienced officer and would be the best guide. As Srivastava stood up to leave and apologized for holding up the minister, Shastri smiled and accompanied him outside, checked whether he had transport arrangements and only on receiving a positive response did he get into his car to leave. Srivastava recalls that in his long association with Shastri, he treated all his guests with the same humility and grace. The advice he got from Shastri in their very first meeting, that the relationship between civil servants and the people should be built on the pillars of mutual respect and regard, remained with him throughout his career.

Srivastava remembers that his next encounter with Shastri was in 1952 in Delhi, when the latter was the railway minister. Srivastava had been to the station to receive his wife and daughter. There was a commotion on the other side of the platform, presumably because another train was arriving, so Srivastava's family decided to wait on the platform until the crowd dispersed. Srivastava soon realized that the large crowd had gathered because Railway Minister Shastri had just arrived on the train entering the platform. Shastri deboarded and started walking away with his officials. However, a few seconds later, he noticed Srivastava standing on the other platform and started walking towards him. Shastri greeted him with folded hands and said, 'Srivastava sahib, namaste. *Aapne mujhe pehchana nahin. Main Lal Bahadur hoon* (You did not recognize me. I am Lal Bahadur).'

Srivastava recalls that he quickly recovered and told Shastri that everyone recognizes him. He went on to add that he was overwhelmed by Shastri's graciousness in remembering him after all these years. Shastri smiled and said that he was aware of Srivastava's posting to Meerut and the good work he was doing. Shastri enquired about his family and well-being and then proceeded to leave after wishing him goodbye. Srivastava felt that it was this ability of Shastri to remember people, recall events related to them and always enquire about their well-being that strengthened their bonds with him.

Shastri's simplicity and unpretentious nature was one of his most enchanting and endearing qualities. This simplicity expressed itself in multiple ways. Firstly, he had no ideological hang-ups or baggage to defend or project. He was seen neither leaning to the Right nor to the Left. This was a huge advantage in those years within the Congress party, as it made him more acceptable to the different factions within the party. When the party was deciding on a successor to Nehru, this absence of any ideological tilt in Shastri played a key role in his emerging as a consensus candidate, and scoring over Morarji. If he was close to any one political position, it was essentially the ideas and principles of Gandhi. As mentioned before, he has often been described as being 'Quintessentially Gandhian' both in his outlook and his approach. Hangen makes a telling point that 'without flaunting his convictions he is probably the most profoundly Gandhian in his attitude towards the world'. While he was strongly influenced by Nehru, in the post-Nehruvian years, one noticed Shastri attempting to carve out an independent space for himself. When criticized for deviating from the Nehruvian path, Shastri asked his critics not to blame Nehru for his (Shastri's) actions, as he would like to take the onus for them.

Shastri's simplicity expressed itself in yet another way. He is often described as being intelligent without having any of the trappings of a typical intellectual. He rarely quoted any writers, philosophers or academics save Gandhi. People found it difficult to 'score over him' as it was impossible to box him in either an ideological slot or intellectual position. His critics would argue that he often got away by taking refuge under the garb of not being an intellectual. Yet, Shastri never attempted to shield himself or his viewpoints using this as an excuse. He was possibly trying to make a much deeper point. His reflections and perceptions were not dictated by any passionate or favoured ideological position but linked to the common Indian's experiences and being firmly embedded in reality. However high he rose in life, he never forgot his humble origins and what it had taught him. This allowed him to keep his ear to the ground. This quality made it possible for him to find solutions to complicated problems, which were often placed in his hands when others failed to find one. This was the source and strength of his simplicity.

There was another facet to his simplicity, which made him a people's person. Shastri was well versed in Hindi and also interspersed it with Urdu. He had a working knowledge of English and was able to convey his viewpoint effectively in it. In whichever language he used, Shastri communicated (both in his written and spoken word) in simple words, free of any hyperbole. His skills were in one-to-one communication, as he had the ability of not just making his point but also giving a patient and respectful audience to what others said. This was an asset of Shastri that the bureaucracy greatly admired. He did not have the oratorical skills of many of his contemporaries but more than made up for that with the simplicity of his words and the passion and earnestness with which he communicated. He did not speak from the head but straight from the heart. While many of his speeches in the Parliament were long and often lacked a punch, he was able to keep the attention of his audience with the honesty of his expressions. His speech in the Lok Sabha, explaining his resignation as railway minister, and his many interventions as HM to draw the attention of the House to the different crisis situations he diffused were not marked by any oratorical brilliance but by a factual, logical and down-to-earth statement of events, facts and solutions.

As PM, the spirited defence of his government when replying to the two NCMs were clear indicators of his steely grit and quiet determination. There were rare occasions when he raised his voice to make a point, especially when it came to defending the government's response to Pakistan's adventurism. Yet, what seemed to matter was the conviction with which he spoke rather than the style that he employed. Shastri also addressed several public rallies as PM, and during the three general elections (1952, 1957 and 1962) as well as with the passage of time, it was clear that his capacity to connect with the audience was instantaneous. Hangen captured this simplicity of Shastri when he said, 'He [Shastri] is nearest to the mind and soil of India. He reflects the strengths and weaknesses of the Indian villager.' As Shastri took over as PM, Hangen was prophetic when he predicted that Shastri could well take his place on the world stage with a vastly magnified stature.[12]

TRULY SECULAR OUTLOOK

It may be useful to dwell for a moment on the influence of the years he spent at Kashi Vidyapeeth. The humanitarian outlook and vision that the Vidyapeeth offered, both in terms of its atmosphere and the specific content of learning, were vital in shaping Shastri's personality and outlook. Three dimensions merit deeper consideration:

- First, the secular credentials that Shastri came to espouse were shaped by the strong influence of his mentor Dr Bhagwan Das, who taught courses on ethics and philosophy at the Vidyapeeth. Dr Das had made a detailed study of all religions. He had written a thesis titled, 'The Essential Unity of All Religions'. In this thesis, he elaborated on the concept of '*samanvayvad*—integration of different points of view'. This principle deeply influenced Shastri.

  At Kashi Vidyapeeth, Shastri wrote his thesis on 'The Philosophy of Dr Bhagwan Das', where he expanded

[12]Hangen, W. "After Nehru, Who?" *Champion of Peace: Tribute to Shastri* by Sudarshan K. Savara, New Delhi: Gyan Mandir 1967, p. 40

on this idea. Shastri was himself not too religious in a ritualistic sense, but retained and maintained a healthy agnosticism. Those who worked with him recall that there were no mandatory temple visits as part of his tour schedules. If he did visit a place of religious significance while on a tour, it was more out of respect for the suggestion of his hosts. Shastri's upholding of the philosophy of integration was best seen in his approach to different religions and their followers. As the HM both in UP and at the national level, Shastri gave top priority to maintaining communal harmony. He played a key role in sensitizing the police in a post-Independence context to their role in preventing the spread of communal tensions and mistrust between communities. His ability to settle complex, ticklish and deeply sensitive religious questions was based on his faith in the essential goodness of all religions and his inclusive approach. Shastri demonstrated through his interactions, how important it was for the leadership at the highest level to give expression to the sentiment of inclusiveness and respect religious diversity.

• Second, the Vidyapeeth also strengthened Shastri's strong faith in the equality of people and the need to avoid caste distinctions and hierarchies. This again became a cardinal principle of his life and strongly reflected in the way he related to people. When introducing himself, he would always say 'Lal Bahadur' and avoid the term 'Shastri', which was not a family name or inheritance but a title attached to his name once he had completed his education at Kashi Vidyapeeth.

• And third, the Vidyapeeth inculcated in Shastri

the spirit of social service. Soon after completing his education there, Shastri joined the SPS and dedicated close to a decade to active social service. He got an opportunity to work with the socially and economically marginalized sections of society. Later, he himself acknowledged that his years in the SPS shaped his attitude not merely towards social service but on how to empathize with people and understand their problems from their perspective. Having grown up in poverty and experienced the challenges that the poor faced, Shastri was, in later years, able to assert the point that 'no one knows more about the pangs of poverty than I do.'[13] In his very first public pronouncement on being elected as the CPP chief, he vowed to fight the twin challenges of poverty and unemployment. His mandate to the Planning Commission too was to add a column in each of its tables on the quantum of employment that each item of expenditure was able to generate.

All those associated with Shastri remember him for the 'trust quotient' he evoked. A former ambassador of the United States (US) to India, John Kenneth Galbraith highlighted this dimension of Shastri: 'There is more iron in his soul than appears on the surface. He listens to every point of view, he makes up his mind firmly, and once he has made them his decisions stick. He is the kind of man who is trusted.'[14]

---

[13]Address to Secretaries of Government of India in August 1964 as quoted in *Lal Bahadur: A Political Biography* by D.R. Mankekar, Bombay: Popular Prakashan, 1964, p. 72. Also, speech at a rally in Calcutta, *The Statesman*, 20 October 1965, from microfilms at NML.

[14]Martin, E.G. & Barnes, J. "Iron in His Soul." *A Study of Lal Bahadur Shastri*, B.S. Gujarati, Delhi: Sterling, 1965, p. 13

It is this trust that made party workers adhere to his guidelines when he was secretary of the Allahabad City Congress, or later as the secretary of the United Provinces Congress Committee and GS of the party at the national level. As he led the party organization both prior to the 1952 and 1957 elections, it was this trust factor that allowed him to bring together factions, agree on a common candidate and resolve what seemed to be irreconcilable differences. CM Pant assigned Shastri the crucial Ministry of Police[15] and Transport in the first post-Independence government in the United Provinces because he trusted Shastri's capability to manage these important portfolios. It was implicit trust that helped him find a solution to the language agitation in Assam, the anti-Hindi agitation in South India, the Hazratbal episode and the Akali agitation.

It was the same implicit trust in his capabilities that made Nehru hand over the MHA to him without hesitation after Pant died, despite the fact that there were other senior ministers eyeing the portfolio and also at a time when the country was beset with a lot of issues. Nehru also handed over sensitive assignments to Shastri, both in the government and within the party. It was the same trust that made Nehru bring Shastri back to the Council of Ministers, as MWP and when an ailing Nehru instructed Shastri, 'You need to do my job', it was again an implicit vote of trust in his abilities. This belief kept getting Shastri back into the Prosperous India and World Without War cabinet after the two occasions when he resigned from the government. His being chosen as the consensus candidate for the position of PM to succeed Nehru

---

[15] It was in 1950 that the police department was put under the Ministry of Home Affairs (MHA).

by the Congress Working Committee (CWC) and the CPP were again a categorical assertion of unqualified trust in his abilities. *The Times*, commenting on Shastri's selection as PM, titled its lead article as 'India turns to a Conciliator'. His strength, the paper said, was his reliance on the politics of compromise and his ability to bind people rather than divide them. It went on to state that Shastri's accession represents a democratization of political leadership. The healthy working relationship that developed between Congress President Kamaraj and PM Shastri was rooted in mutual trust.

As PM, Shastri always took the Parliament and members of the Opposition into confidence. He made all important policy announcements in the Parliament and demonstrated his respect for institutions. He rarely missed sessions of the House and made it a point to be present in important debates. This is in stark contrast to the current times, when ministers usually do not make the Parliament and its deliberations a top priority. Shastri held frequent discussions with leaders of the Opposition and briefed them on major political developments and initiatives. This possibly explains why the deliberations of the House during his time were largely free of any rancour and aggressive confrontation. The trust he built up with political leaders across the political spectrum was a key factor that contributed to his greater acceptability.

During the conflict on the borders with Pakistan, both the Army as well as the Air Force chiefs have stated on record that they were able to achieve what they did because of the mutual trust they shared with the PM. At the various stages of the Tashkent talks, trust was a key factor in Shastri, Kosygin and Khan being able to arrive at a consensus that became part of the accord. Shastri was also convinced that whatever misgivings the leaders of the Opposition parties had about the agreement could be addressed by him in one-to-one conversations on his return to India. That was never to happen, but Shastri was confident as he signed the agreement that his fellow citizens and his political contemporaries would trust the sincerity of his intentions.

HIGH STANDARDS IN PROBITY

The trust that people had in Shastri was also on account of his commitment to principles, rules and regulations. Whenever he occupied a position in the government, he ensured that there was no scope for any complaint about not just him but also any of his family members. He made sure that none of his relations would be in a position where they could be accused of misusing their position or proximity to him. His son, Anil, recalled an incident when he was fifteen years old.[16] He was extremely fond of driving and though he had not yet attained the age that made him eligible to get a driving licence, he had learnt to drive. He decided to seek the help of Shastri's office staff to secure a licence even before attaining the age of eligibility. Shastri's additional private secretary contacted the transport department and the licence-issuing authority, and secured a driving licence for Anil the very same day. When Anil proudly announced this to his father, Shastri looked perturbed, hurt and upset. He summoned the additional private secretary who had helped his son secure the licence and made it clear that it was a violation of rules and something he would never approve of. Shastri sent a message to the ministry asking for the concerned Road Transport Office to be held accountable. Shastri felt that the law of the land had been

---

[16]Choudary, P. & Shastri, A. (2015). *Lal Bahadur Shastri: Lessons in Leadership*, Delhi: Wisdom Village Publications, pp. 46–7

flouted in the PM's own house, which, for him, was a matter of deep concern.

He pointed out two important violations. Firstly, the licence was issued to someone who was not eligible in terms of age. Secondly, it was issued without a driving test. Not only did he get the issue of the driving licence rescinded, but also wanted corrective action taken in the department to hold officers accountable for such lapses and prevent its recurrence. Anil was also spoken to at length about the implications of what he had done and how it went against the core values that Shastri stood for. He wanted a clear message to be sent that bending rules to favour those in power would never be acceptable to him. This was the high standard that he had set for himself.

Today, one often finds that the access to power is a passport to violate and sidestep norms. More often than not, those in power are approached by people, not to get a legitimate job done but to use one's authority to bend the rules. The discretionary powers that the authorities enjoy have become a major source of the violation of norms, favouritism and nepotism. In the two decades that Shastri occupied important positions within the government, he was clear that primacy needs to be accorded to following the norms. This greatly enhanced the quantum of trust that people reposed in him.

Linked to the trust quotient was his virtue of consistency. Officers who worked with him found it easy to take forward his instructions, as he stood by his word. Many misinterpreted Shastri's consistency as his overdependence on the bureaucracy. There are several instances when he went against the advice of senior civil servants, but took them into confidence before making his final decision. While resolving the Hazratbal controversy, he decided to go against the advice tendered by the Union home secretary, but kept him in the loop. On his first foreign mission to ease tensions with Nepal, he did not concur with the line suggested by the Indian ambassador but maintained an element of consistency in his position. This approach was greatly respected and appreciated by the bureaucracy.

Even his colleagues in the Cabinet admired Shastri for his consistency. As PM, he backed his ministers in decisions that they took, as long as they conformed to the broader framework laid down by the government. Chidambaram Subramaniam, who was handpicked by Shastri to be the food and agriculture minister, recalls the strong support he got from the PM in Cabinet meetings, to deal with the food crisis. Once Shastri gave his consent to an initiative or a line of action, he would support his Cabinet colleagues and the bureaucracy to take it forward and defend them as and when necessary. Many vital decisions that had to be made during the food crisis were opposed by senior ministers in Cabinet meetings. Shastri helped colleagues gain support for the steps to be taken once he was convinced that those measures were necessary to further the policy goals.

Shastri was also deeply committed to putting processes in place to fight corruption within the administration. As Union HM, he got the Santhanam Committee appointed to suggest strategies to tackle corruption. The committee was given a free hand to make recommendations. It submitted its report during Shastri's prime ministership and he ensured that some of the important recommendations of the committee, especially on the accountability of civil servants, were implemented. Similarly, as HM, he was keen on setting up a high-level commission to suggest administrative reforms on the lines of the Hoover Commission in the US. Soon after becoming

PM, he constituted a high-powered Administrative Reforms Commission headed by Morarji, and gave it a wide area of reference and a specific mandate to suggest comprehensive and overarching reforms in the administrative system at multiple levels.

During the conflict with Pakistan, the decision to take the battle into Pakistani territory was taken after prolonged discussions. Once the decision was made, Shastri gave clear instructions to the military commanders to take it forward logically. Later, at the Tashkent talks, Shastri had detailed deliberations with his ministerial colleagues, senior officers and military commanders on the stand to be taken on withdrawing from the Haji Pir Pass. Once he secured their consent, he ensured that the line he took was consistent with the consensus arrived at. This approach allowed Shastri to carry all sections with him in supporting the implementation of decisions.

A 'PEOPLE'S PERSON'

A key element that contributed to Shastri's success as a leader and revered public figure was his unbounded patience. Commenting on this unique virtue of Shastri, veteran journalist Frank Moraes once observed that Shastri was not easily ruffled.[17] His patience was monumental and seemed inexhaustible. 'Lal Bahadur is too self-effacing to be burdened with the consciousness of history,' Moraes said. Often referred to as a 'synthesiswallah', Shastri's innate skills lay in bringing together diverse factions and approaches and reconciling their differences to arrive at a consensus. It

---

[17]Moraes, F. (1964, June 10). Man of Peace and Principle. *The Indian Express.*

was this quality of Shastri that endeared him to Nehru right from the time the two worked together at the Allahabad City Congress Committee. His capacity to ensure a formula acceptable to all sections made him the favourite of Congress workers and leaders in the first three general elections. On the two occasions when he left the Cabinet, his services were immediately utilized for party work. He went across the country resolving local disputes within the Congress and helping iron out differences. He was much sought after by Congress CMs and state party unit presidents as a bridge between the state and the national unit. As HM, Shastri had developed an excellent rapport with the CMs (most of whom hailed from the Congress party) and later encashed this goodwill when the consensus-building emerged to choose the successor to Nehru.

Moraes makes another important point, that 'there is always a window open in his [Shastri's] mind.' This provided opportunities for considering multiple viewpoints and at the negotiating table, each one felt that their voice was heard and respected and that they had an important takeaway from the meeting with Shastri. Commenting on his own capacity to reconcile different viewpoints, Shastri conceded, 'I can carry everyone along with me. That is much better... This approach may delay decisions a little, but that does not bother me at all. It is a price worth paying.' Journalist Welles Hangen also observed, '[There is] considerably more guile in the little man that his mild manner indicates... [The] appearance of mediocrity is often an advantage for a politician.' This was typical of the style adopted by Shastri.

As PM, one of the initial criticisms against Shastri was the delays in decision-making, procrastination and an excessive amount of time and energy spent on what was termed as unnecessary deliberations. This was very much the focus of the first NCM against the Shastri government. Shastri defended his style by asserting that in a democracy, constant consultations and the free expression of views must precede decision-making. Vijaya Lakshmi Pandit, who had derided Shastri, now complimented him along with other leaders on the swiftness of his decision-making after the war with Pakistan. During this conflict, those who worked closely with Shastri were pleasantly surprised at the extraordinary speed and strength of his reactions and decisions. A co-worker who had observed him from close quarters hinted that only a crisis could bring out Shastri's true qualities. When the situation demanded a quick response, Shastri seemed prepared for the same, though the process of consultation and arriving at a consensus continued to be his favoured mode of decision-making.

Two of Shastri's early mentors, Purushottam Das (P.D.) Tandon and G.B. Pant, highlighted the skills that Shastri brought to decision-making. Tandon referred to Shastri as a genius in striking a balance, handling difficult situations and achieving compromises.[18] He went on to add that behind Shastri's humility, there was a 'rock of toughness' that made him an effective negotiator and decision-maker. Pant highlighted five qualities that Shastri possessed: likeable, hardworking, devoted, trustworthy and non-controversial. All these qualities made it possible for him to be a successful peacemaker and problem-solver. Shastri's style of action is what made him a favourite choice. He would quietly do things, without much fanfare or drawing public attention. This quiet efficiency was

---

[18]Natesan, M. "Prime Minister Lal Bahadur Shastri." *A Study of Lal Bahadur Shastri*, B.S. Gujarati, Delhi: Sterling, 1965, p. 52.

what contributed to his appeal and acceptance.

Michael Brecher powerfully summarized the impact of the unique qualities that Shastri possessed, when he said that 'the combination of the qualities of humility, patience, respect for conflicting viewpoints, sensitivity to powerful emotional currents, along with subtlety and quiet firmness' made him the most sought after leader to resolve differences between diverse groups and opinions.[19] He was truly a person who may have looked soft on the outside but had a steely determination and was tough from within.

Many contemporaries of Shastri, such as Morarji, Vengalil Krishnan (V.K.) Krishna Menon, Tiruvellore Thattai (T.T.) Krishnamachari and Jagjivan Ram, believed that Shastri's strength lay in the confidence that his mentors had in him. It was argued that Shastri was always in the shadow of these mentors and moved up the ladder of power on account of their support and guidance. P.D. Tandon was a guide during his initial years in the SPS. Later, when Shastri joined the United Provinces government, CM Pant took on the role of his mentor (and critics would add, protector). And when he moved to Delhi, Nehru was his guide, whose instructions and directions he implicitly followed.

During Nehru's prime ministership, in the corridors of power, there was talk of two tactics that Shastri would employ. First, he would mention that a particular course of action was in keeping with what Jawaharlal Nehru wished. The second tactic would be to allow rival sides to argue out their points and exhaust their energies. Shastri would then move in and strike a compromise position to which all would

---

[19]Brecher, M. (1966). *Succession in India: A Study in Decision-making.* Oxford University Press. p. 93

agree. When Nehru passed away and the consultation process began within the Congress for the choice of a successor, the whispers included, 'Who will Shastri now consult, if asked who should be PM?'

Even if one were to concede that Shastri was strongly influenced by his mentors at different stages of his life, he emerged from their shadows when he became the PM. It would truly be an overstatement to say that he was nothing without his mentors. In a power hierarchy, it may well be normal for a political leader to act with deference to those senior to them, more so when one is accountable to them. This could have been true in Shastri's case too. Yet, this did not imply that he did not express his independent views even with these mentors. *The Times*, in its assessment of Shastri, highlighted that he was, for long, involved in 'quiet innovation, independent action and impressive but not always publicised success'[20]; it was unlikely for him to be restricted to always being in someone else's shadow.

There are enough indications of Shastri clarifying his stand with Nehru, be it on India's unpreparedness during the attack by China, the continuation of V.K. Krishna Menon in the Cabinet, the removal of Keshav Dev Malviya as a minister on corruption charges, recommending action against Punjab CM Partap Singh Kairon, getting Pattom A. Thanu Pillai appointed as governor or resolving the anti-Hindi agitation. In all these decisions taken by Nehru, the influence of Shastri's stand and position was apparent. Yet, Shastri weighed his options and preferred to bide his time. When he knew that as MWP, he was not given the type of role that Nehru had promised ('You have to do my work' was what Nehru had told him soon after

---

[20]14 June 1964. From microfilms at NML.

he fell ill during the Bhubaneswar session of the Congress), he did not protest. When files approved by him were vetted by Indira Gandhi, he preferred to remain silent. When senior officers went straight to Nehru and reversed decisions he had suggested, he preferred to keep quiet. When the discussion on the successor to Nehru began, he met Indira Gandhi and only when he was sure that she was not keen on the PM's position, did he allow his name to be suggested. While some may see this as a weakness, others would view it as political shrewdness. While confrontation was not his style, he preferred to allow events and decisions to take their natural course. Supporters of Shastri viewed this as one of his important strengths. His opponents, on the other hand, saw it as a serious drawback and weakness. Half a century after his passing away, when one reflects on his career and achievements, it appears as if his approach of seeking common ground rather than moving on the path of confrontation was the key to his many successes.

The quote of Guru Nanak that always adorned his desk summed up Shastri's philosophy and work ethic, 'O Nanak! Be tiny like the grass, for other plants will wither away, but grass will remain ever green'. *The Times* summed up the qualities of Shastri in its assessment of the new leadership that emerged in India after the passing away of Nehru as thus:

> His meekness is protective colouring for a calm, unhurried, self-confidence combined with good judgment and a shrewd political sense... [His] qualities of self-effacement may enhance his standing among those Indians who regard ambition as degrading and power as corrupting, safe only in the hands of a man who does not seek it but has it thrust upon him.

The above narration outlines the distinctiveness of the style and approach that Shastri displayed during his political career and public life that spanned over four decades. A few terms are integral to Shastri's approach and define him as an individual. His unflinching commitment to principles, rules and regulations were the foundation stones for the trust that people reposed in him. His work ethic, which involved a demonstration of remarkable levels of energy, attention to detail, a rigorous process of consultation and, above all, seeking a win-win situation, established a benchmark in being dedicated to the task assigned. This has very few parallels among his predecessors or his successors. His transparent humility and rare simplicity became an object of animated debate, but at the end of the day, even his most bitter critics had to concede that humility was his honest, natural trait and his simplicity was no act to score brownie points.

Shastri's quiet approach to decision-making and problem-solving was shorn of any effort to attract public attention or showing off. His strength lay in his substance and not in his style. Rather than any display of flamboyance, his actions demonstrated his earnestness and won public appreciation. This understated approach was often mistaken as a weakness and excessive dependence on his mentors. Often, this impression may have been a byproduct of the sharp differences in his personality as compared to that of his mentors. Nehru was charismatic and a larger-than-life figure. G.B. Pant was a towering personality both in terms of his physical stature and style. This 'Lion of Kumaon' commanded attention and respect for this reason. Shastri on the other hand, with his measured tone and self-effacing nature, was quite the opposite and was admired for these very qualities. His leadership style was truly a study in contrast, which, over time, produced the same degree of effectiveness.

As a people's person, Shastri's strengths lay in his calm assertiveness, capacity to win friends and developing a consensus approach to decision-making. This approach was distinctly different from his predecessor (Nehru) and often resulted in the drawing of comparisons. An assessment of Shastri the individual, his principles and politics would lead one to conclude that he needs to be evaluated not in comparison to others but in the specific historical context in which he made his mark and the unique style and innovation he brought to his own brand of leadership.

2

GROUNDED IN LOCAL REALITY

It has often been stressed that in public life, the higher one rises in stature and position, the more important it is that they be firmly grounded in reality. Lal Bahadur Shastri's life provides a classic example of success in public life being rooted in experience of public service and political activity at the local level. In the early 1920s, Shastri was influenced by the call of Mahatma Gandhi to enter the freedom movement, while still in his teens. The next three decades of his involvement in public/political activity was the foundation for his transition to national politics.

Shastri's early years were filled with hardships and challenges. Born in Mughalsarai into a poor Kayastha family in 1904, he lost his father when he was just a year and a half old. He remained under the care of his mother and maternal grandfather. He was required to change towns and schools after his primary education and he moved to live with his maternal uncle. He was known among his classmates to be a hard-working and conscientious student, though not necessarily brilliant.

During his school days, many incidents are indicative of the sterling qualities that he possessed, which played a significant role in shaping his actions and attitudes when he entered public life and politics. A story from his childhood is frequently quoted. As a six-year-old, he went to an orchard with his friends. While the friends all climbed trees to pluck fruits, Lal Bahadur remained on the ground and decided to pluck a rose. The gardener admonished him and Lal Bahadur began to weep, saying, 'Don't scold me as my father died when I was a year and a half old.' The gardener sympathized with him and advised him that it was all the more important that he exhibit better behaviour and not take anything without the owner's permission. This incident left a lasting impression on Lal Bahadur and right conduct became the central value he came to practise.

In primary school, he was once punished by his teacher for not bringing to class an English book as per the instructions. The fact was that Lal Bahadur's financial means did not allow him to purchase the book and he used to borrow it from classmates and take notes from them as and when needed. Lal Bahadur quietly accepted the punishment. His principle was clear—make that extra effort to complete the task assigned and not make deprivation an excuse. Much later when in high school, he often swam across the river to reach his school as he did not want to seek anyone's favour to sponsor a boat ride. He would very diplomatically move away from his classmates when the boat approached, in order not to cause any embarrassment either to them or to him.

An incident during his school days merits recalling. One of his teachers was Nishkameshwar Misra. Strongly patriotic in his vision and intensely humane in his approach, Misra regaled the class with stories of Maharana Pratap, Rani Laxmibai, Shivaji, Gopal Krishna Gokhale, Bipin Chandra Pal, Lala Lajpat Rai, Bal Gangadhar Tilak and Sri Aurobindo, among others. Lal Bahadur's family did not have any visible nationalistic background and none of the elders in the family had been involved in the struggle for freedom. Misra's classes and anecdotes had a strong bearing on Lal Bahadur. Misra was also greatly impressed by Shastri's diligence, discipline and dedication. He was appointed as class monitor and coordinated all the extracurricular activities. On realizing that Lal Bahadur was absenting himself from these after-school activities because of his financial situation, Misra decided to pay on his behalf. He also took him home, where he and his wife treated him like a son.

Shastri's biographer C.P. Srivastava records another interesting episode linked to Lal Bahadur's school days. Aware of Lal Bahadur's financial challenges, Misra asked him to tutor one of his young children. Knowing that he would refuse to take any remuneration for this, Misra placed the money every month in a savings box. Several years later, Lal Bahadur's sister was getting married; Misra handed over the money from the savings box to Lal Bahadur's mother and explained to her that this was his legitimate earning. This amount helped immensely to prepare for the wedding.

As a young student, Lal Bahadur enjoyed reading. His early education had been in Urdu and he later learnt Hindi. When he spoke, his speech was always a mix of Hindi and Urdu. Besides well-known writers in both the languages, the works and words of Tilak and Lala Lajpat Rai also influenced him deeply. In 1915, as a student, he heard Gandhi speak in Benaras. The sincerity of his words and the simplicity of his personality had a lasting impression on Lal Bahadur. As a 'Quintessential Gandhian', L.P. Singh believes that Shastri carried forward three 'sterling virtues' from his adolescence— 'patriotism, a readiness to take risks, and self-denial'—which shaped his personality and approach to life.[21]

---

[21]Singh, L.P. (1996). *Portrait of Lal Bahadur Shastri: A Quintessential Gandhian*. Ravi Dayal Publisher, p. 6

In life, he would have many opportunities to prove his patriotic fervour, capacity to take risks and trademark self-restraint. These verily became his 'calling cards'.

THE MAHATMA'S INFLUENCE

In January 1921, as a Class X student, he got another chance to hear the Mahatma at a meeting held at Benaras. This meeting was conducted just after the Congress party's December 1920 annual session at Nagpur. The party had decided to intensify the Non-cooperation Movement. At the meeting in Benaras, Gandhi made a special appeal, unmindful of its consequences, to the youth above sixteen to withdraw from government-aided or -controlled educational institutions, and join the freedom movement. Another well-known stalwart of those days, Madan Mohan Malaviya had chaired that meeting. In his speech, Malaviya reminded the youngsters to take a decision on quitting their education and joining the freedom movement only after speaking to their parents and getting their consent.

The young Lal Bahadur, who had attended the meeting with his friends, was deeply influenced by the Mahatma's words. He was also mindful of what Malaviya had said. He was aware that completing the Class X examination would be a passport to securing a stable job. Given the financial constraints his family faced and their dependence on him, he was caught in a dilemma. He ultimately went by his mother's advice, who told him to consider all dimensions of any action he proposed to take, make a firm resolve and strictly adhere to it. He pondered over the matter and as per his mother's advice, decided that the country needed his services and it was his duty to make any sacrifice that was warranted. He discontinued his school education and joined the Congress party as a volunteer. This change of track by heeding to the call of his conscience was a familiar trait that Shastri was to demonstrate when he reached interesting crossroads later in his life.

In the life and actions of Shastri, his mother's advice remained with him till the very end and was a key mantra that guided all his actions. The Mahatma also remained an important influence and shaped his ideals and principles.

Over the next two decades, Shastri actively participated in the activities of the Congress party and was even jailed many times. He was arrested first for his participation in the Non-cooperation Movement, then during the Salt Satyagraha in the 1930s and during the Quit India Movement in the '40s. Shastri kept himself busy in jail by reading and talking to people. As mentioned earlier, during his different jail terms, he was an important influence over his jail mates and often resolved their squabbles and disputes.

During one of his jail terms, his daughter fell seriously ill and he was given parole for two weeks. Soon after he reached home, his daughter died and after completing the ceremonies, he decided to return to jail. When told that the parole was for two weeks, he averred that the parole was to look after his daughter and now that she was no more, he would go back to jail. This was a clear indicator of his integrity and his commitment to principles. Later, on another occasion, when Shastri was in jail, his son fell seriously ill. He was granted parole to spend time with his ailing son, but throughout the duration of the parole, his son's temperature showed no sign of going down. Though his son was in tears seeing his father return to jail, Shastri did not relent and merely patted him before leaving. His family members also asked him to apply for an extension of the parole, but he refused and went back to jail.

In February 1921, Gandhi inaugurated Kashi Vidyapeeth. Having made an emotional appeal to young people to quit government-aided educational institutions, the Mahatma was keen to provide those who had discontinued their education and joined his movement with an alternative stream of learning. When a businessman and philanthropist, Shiv Prasad Gupta took the initiative to start Kashi Vidyapeeth, Gandhi agreed to be present at the opening ceremony. Lal Bahadur too was there at the inaugural function and decided to enrol for the four-year course that would lead to the 'Shastri' degree[22]. While at the Kashi Vidyapeeth, Lal Bahadur came under the strong influence of Dr Bhagwan Das, one of the academicians at the Vidyapeeth. Lal Bahadur preferred to study philosophy and ethics. The influence of the ideas of Dr Das was patently visible in the inclusive outlook to people and politics that was to be the hallmark of Shastri's approach.

Till the 1940s, the learning at Kashi Vidyapeeth focused not so much on intellectual development but on practical learning. This possibly explains Shastri's approach to problems, which was strongly rooted in practical considerations rather than anchored in any visible ideological/theoretical nuances. Further, the fact that Shastri's formal education was all in India, is reflected in the idioms he used, examples he made and ideas he espoused. In his speeches, he rarely quoted from any celebrated writers and thinkers save for Gandhi. In the years ahead, the marked difference in the approach of Shastri and his many contemporaries, who had the opportunity to study in England, was evident in the content of their public

---

[22]This degree was later recognized as being equivalent to the Bachelor of Arts.

pronouncements. While Shastri's was strongly rooted in local philosophy and his life experience, those who benefitted from Western education invariably provided proof of the same in both the content and style of their public speeches.

In 1926, after completing his studies from Kashi Vidyapeeth and even as he was active as a Congress volunteer, Shastri enrolled in the SPS. This society had been started by Lala Lajpat Rai in 1921. Shastri was familiar with the writings of Rai ever since his school days and they had left a deep impression on him. The SPS trained the young to develop a 'nationalistic outlook', committed to social work and national transformation. He was interviewed by Rai and was sent to Muzaffarnagar district of the United Provinces for field work. Impressed with Shastri's service and dedication, Rai made him a probationary member of the society a year later, in 1927. In 1928, Rai passed away and the presidentship of the society passed on to P.D. Tandon. Shastri was assigned to work with him at the society's office in Allahabad. This was the start of a long association between the two.

Shastri was strongly influenced by Tandon. Later, Tandon was to comment that behind Shastri's humility, there was a 'rock of toughness' and he was a genius in 'striking balances, handling difficult situations and achieving compromises'.[23] Shastri's sensitivity towards the problems and challenges faced by the underprivileged was clearly evident in the work he did while at the society. This was an important foundation for the many public responsibilities he would shoulder in the years ahead. In 1930, Shastri was conferred the life membership of the SPS.

---

[23]Natesan, M. "Prime Minister Lal Bahadur Shastri." *A Study of Lal Bahadur Shastri*, B.S. Gujarati, Delhi: Sterling, 1965, p. 52

During his time in the SPS, Shastri also got married to Lalita Devi in 1927. He insisted on a simple wedding ceremony. The only gift that she brought over from her parental home was a spinning wheel and a few yards of khadi. Over the years, his wife became a pillar of support and stood by him in all his commitments to public activity and political life. She was strongly influenced by his value system and patriotic fervour and practised the same in her life too. His family members recall an interesting incident involving Devi and their eldest daughter, Kusum.[24] When Kusum was six years old, there was an exhibition (mela) that came to their town. Devi was keen that they all go to the exhibition, but Shastri was hesitant, as he could not afford the exhibition's entrance fees. Devi then borrowed ₹25 from a friend and went to the exhibition with Shastri and their daughter.

They moved around the exhibition and whenever Kusum expressed a wish to buy something, Shastri politely refused permission. When, on returning home, Devi felt bad that they were not able to buy anything for their daughter, Shastri's message to his wife (and daughter) was simple and straightforward:

> I know that you are angry because nothing has been purchased by you from the exhibition. It was deliberately done, because you had borrowed money from one of your friends. It looks very odd that we should buy something with the borrowed money. You should hereafter keep in mind that unless it is absolutely necessary to purchase a thing, we should not borrow money.

---

[24]Choudary, P. & Shastri, A. (2015). *Lal Bahadur Shastri: Lessons in Leadership*, Delhi: Wisdom Village Publications, pp. 46–7

Family members recall that since this incident, Devi never borrowed money from anyone, even if it was for an urgent matter.

There is yet another interesting episode connected to his membership of the SPS and his family. Shastri used to receive ₹50 a month from the society to meet household expenses. Once, when serving a jail term, he was concerned whether the money was reaching his family and was sufficient for their sustenance. His wife assured him that the amount was sufficient and she was actually saving ₹10 every month. Shastri promptly wrote a letter to the society, asking them to reduce the payment to ₹40, saying that it was sufficient and that the other ₹10 be given to the family of any other freedom fighter who may be in need of it. This was yet another proof of Shastri's high ethical standards and larger societal vision.

COMMITMENT ABOVE ALL ELSE

During one of his jail terms, Shastri came to know that his wife was not keeping good health. He wrote to her, asking her to drink a glass of milk every day. Devi did not want to let Shastri know the difficult financial conditions she was facing. She decided to do as Shastri wished, but consumed the milk in a very small glass meant for a toddler. She wrote back to Shastri that she was consuming a glass of milk every day and encouraged him to continue his agitation against foreign rule. Shastri came to know of the actual quantity of milk that his wife consumed only after he was released from jail. For him, the stand and action taken by his wife reflected her commitment to speak the truth and also support his agitation.

Shastri's experiences of managing people and their problems while working with the SPS played a central role in shaping his approach to politics. C.P. Srivastava, who worked closely with him as a civil servant, highlights that Shastri had the 'capacity to feel and think like the decent common people of India.' L.P. Singh, another officer who saw Shastri from close quarters, maintains that the 'virtue of consistency' was his biggest quality. He did what he said and his strength was his 'practical judgement' and not any 'intellectual learning.' These qualities were clearly the byproducts of the key learnings from his initial years in public service.

Shastri himself reflected on the years he was with the society, and its impact. He believed that it was 'due to my membership of the society that I got an opportunity to serve my country the most. The society has inculcated in me the meaning of the term "Servants of the People."'[25] Shastri's sense of fairness, equity and justice were clearly honed during his years of work with the society.

It must, however, be stressed that incidents from his childhood clearly indicated the firmness of resolve and sense of fairness that he always believed in. Possibly, the experience of working with the SPS only further strengthened those core values. It is reported that once in his younger days, he had gone out for a walk in Mirzapur with his maternal uncle. They passed an old man who was carrying a sack of mangoes. The elderly gentleman told Lal Bahadur and his uncle that he was returning home and was keen to dispose the mangoes left over. He was willing to sell hundred mangoes for 4 paise, which was half the rate he would normally sell it for. The old man was handed over 4 paise and he started counting the mangoes. When he reached fifty, Lal Bahadur asked him to stop. Even

[25]Singh, L.P. (1996). *Portrait of Lal Bahadur Shastri: A Quintessential Gandhian.* Ravi Dayal Publisher

though the old man said that he has to give fifty more, Lal Bahadur told him that they needed only fifty mangoes. On continuing their stroll, the maternal uncle told him that he had been foolish in allowing the elderly man to keep the fifty mangoes that were due to them. Lal Bahadur immediately rationalized that, 'it was a distress sale. Why take advantage of such a situation?'[26] This sense of fairness got further honed while he worked for the SPS and became the cornerstone of his dealings with people.

Shastri's adherence to his conviction of what was right was his biggest asset. He had demonstrated this quality in his younger days itself. Shastri's maternal uncle enjoyed having non-vegetarian food once in a way, though Shastri himself was a strict vegetarian. At their Mughalsarai house, the uncle would occasionally bring a bird to be cooked for dinner. One day, a pigeon sat on the terrace and the uncle asked Lal Bahadur to go fetch the bird. Anticipating what his uncle was likely to do, Lal Bahadur refused to accede to his request. His uncle then assured the boy that he would not kill the bird. In all sincerity, Lal Bahadur did catch the pigeon and handed it over to the uncle, who promptly got the pigeon cooked. Lal Bahadur was so upset that he went on a hunger strike. He was soon joined by the women in the family. In the face of this protest, his uncle promised never to consume non-vegetarian food again. Lal Bahadur broke his fast and his uncle too kept his promise. In a way, this was Shastri's first satyagraha!

Between 1930 and 1936, Shastri served as the GS and later president of the Allahabad District Congress Committee. The office was located at Anand Bhawan, the Nehru family home.

[26]Choudary, P. & Shastri, A. (2015). *Lal Bahadur Shastri: Lessons in Leadership*, Delhi: Wisdom Village Publications, pp. 7–8

This gave him an opportunity to frequently interact with Nehru, who was to be his mentor in later days. Commenting on their relationship, Shastri said[27]:

> [Whenever] Jawaharlalji got an opportunity; he gave me full scope for work. At his instance, I held office of the Secretary and President of the District and City Committees at Allahabad in the thirties. When he became President of the United Provinces Congress Committee he made me the General Secretary... He has some faith in me that I would do well in any task entrusted to me.

This period was thus critical in the political life of Shastri, as it paved the way for his active involvement in the party and government in the subsequent decades.

In 1937, Shastri was elected to the United Provinces Assembly from a constituency in Allahabad. A major task he completed during this time on behalf of the Congress party was the drafting of a report on the zamindari system and land reforms. His concern for the landless poor and his understanding of the landholding pattern in India was reflected in the report that he produced. When the Congress assumed power in the province, they soon introduced legislations to give effect to the contents of the report. This report also became the basis of the land reforms that were introduced in other states in post-Independence India.

It is clear that in each of the activities that he undertook, be it as a volunteer at the SPS or as an office bearer in the city, district and provincial Congress Committee or as an

---

[27]Mankekar, D.R. (1965). *Lal Bahadur: A Political Biography*. Bombay: Popular Prakashan, p. 77

elected member of the Provincial Assembly, he left a lasting impact through the initiatives he piloted. His sincerity and dedication became his visiting cards and they were the core of his attitude and approach. There was more to come in terms of his contribution to the United Provinces in the years ahead.

POLITICAL LIFE

In 1945, as the provinces were preparing for an election, Shastri was appointed as the secretary to the United Provinces Parliamentary Board of the Congress. Nehru was then its president. Shastri, as secretary, was responsible for the choice of candidates for the election and developing a strategy for winning the maximum number of seats. Given the factionalism in the party, Shastri's task was why of a reconciler and recommending the appropriate person to be given the party ticket. This was the specific reason why Nehru had entrusted him with that responsibility. Shastri did justice to his task and resolved many a dispute on selecting candidates. The Congress won a resounding victory in the elections and Shastri himself was elected to the Provincial legislature from Allahabad. It must be said to Shastri's credit that for his work as the secretary of the Parliamentary Board of the Congress party in this large province, he won the admiration and support of all sections of Congress leaders and workers for his impartial approach and sense of fair play. This was to remain his biggest strength and asset in his political career.

A year before Independence, in 1946, he was appointed as the parliamentary secretary to CM G.B. Pant in the United Provinces. Given Shastri's proximity to P.D. Tandon, Pant hoped that bringing Shastri in as the parliamentary secretary would help him gauge and relate to what Tandon's expectations from the government and its leadership were. Further, when Pant was scouting for candidates for the position of parliamentary secretary, he had several names to choose from. Shastri was the only one about whom there were no negative comments! Shastri's yen for hard work was evident in this assignment as parliamentary secretary. He often stayed on in the office late into the night. Pant followed a similar schedule and both would often end up driving back home together in Pant's car. This also gave an opportunity to Pant to experience Shastri's discipline and hard work, and brought them very close. During these formative years in public office, Pant was an important influence on Shastri and was one of his key mentors.

With the dawn of Independence, Shastri joined the United Provinces Cabinet of Pant as the minister for police and transport. Pant and Shastri were both 'workaholics' and further developed a strong working relationship during these days. The work ethic that Shastri maintained greatly impressed and influenced Pant.

Shastri held the portfolio of police and transport for four years, before being called to the Centre to assume charge as GS of the Congress party. During these four years, Shastri laid the foundation for a robust police administration and an effective transport network. The choice of portfolios that Pant decided to assign Shastri was indicative of the CM's expectations from Shastri. In the years after Independence, both these portfolios would be vital in representing the transformation from an administration under colonial rule to one under an independent democratic polity accountable to its citizens.

When Shastri assumed charge as a minister, government officials visited his home and installed an air conditioner in it. When he returned home in the evening, his children told him of this development with great excitement. Shastri immediately asked the concerned officials to remove the air conditioner. He called his children and told them, 'This ministership is not permanent. When Father's job is gone, you will still have to live in an ordinary home without air conditioning. So, if we don't get used to these comforts, we will not be in trouble later.'[28] The children understood the value of their father's advice. Later in life too, Shastri occupied several important positions. He was always quick to ensure that the privileges that go with a position were not taken for granted and the family was always grounded in reality.

Once, when Shastri came to know that one of his children had taken the office car for a drive, he summoned the official who worked at his home to calculate the petrol costs that that ride involved and made a payment for the same. He also counselled the children that the official privileges were not for the use of the family and they should desist from doing so.

Drawing the boundary line between what constitutes the legitimate privileges of enjoying a public office on the one hand and the misuse of the same was something that Shastri was mindful of. This line of distinction has today got increasingly blurred and, in the case of many holders of public office, does not even seem to exist! Shastri's approach to public life, especially when he was a minister, provides an example of how a public servant needs to approach the privileges that come with a position. Shastri often erred on the side of perfection, as he did not wish to give a hint of an opportunity to anyone to raise questions about his integrity and ethical standards.

---

[28]Prasad, K.B.R. (2017). *Office of the Indian Prime Minister: Lal Bahadur Shastri Period*. Chennai: Notion press, p. 14

WINNING FRIENDS, INFLUENCING PEOPLE

Shastri's principal task as minister for police was to transform the outlook of the police from a colonial security apparatus to an efficient post-Independence law-and-order administrative system. Towards this end of transforming the police from an instrument of repression to a vehicle of protection, he made every effort to reorient the attitude of officers and the larger police force. Over the years, it has been found that the police (home) portfolio often makes ministers very unpopular. As the first police minister of the largest province of Independent India, Shastri set exacting standards with his 'citizen-friendly' approach. These continue to be the benchmark even today.

Shastri enjoyed watching cricket matches and an interesting episode during his tenure as HM is often quoted. There was a match between India and England being played at the Green Park Stadium at Kanpur. Shastri went to watch the match. During the match, there was some commotion in a stand reserved for university students. On hearing the noise, Shastri decided to go and enquire about the problem himself. The students told him that they would allow play to resume only when the 'khaki uniforms were out of their sight'. Shastri promised them that the 'khaki uniforms will be out of their sight the next day' and the play resumed.[29]

The next day, there was further commotion at the student pavilion. Shastri again enquired from the students what their problem was. They brought to his attention that they had been assured the previous day that the police would not be around but they were present in larger numbers! Shastri smilingly replied that they had been assured that there 'won't

---

[29]Choudary, P. & Shastri, A. (2015). *Lal Bahadur Shastri: Lessons in Leadership*, Delhi: Wisdom Village Publications, p. 60

be any policemen in khaki uniform... (today) they are in white uniforms.' The students realized that they had been outfoxed by a witty Shastri. They enjoyed a good laugh and the match went on peacefully. This was quite typical of Shastri's style of winning friends and not creating any enemies. Over time, it got more sophisticated in terms of its techniques and strategies, and paid much bigger dividends!

A major reform in the police that he introduced was prohibiting the use of lathis in the first instance, when dealing with law-and-order challenges. He replaced the lathi with a water hose. The principle underlying this reform was clear. In post-Independence India, the immediate use of violence by the police against citizens should, as far as possible, be avoided. The water hose would help disperse a mob going out of control, while not causing major physical injuries to protestors. What was started by Shastri in UP, later spread to other states of the country.

Shastri also adopted firm measures to curb communal violence. Given the fact that the United Provinces faced challenges in the post-Partition period on account of migration and refugees, and was also regarded as a communally sensitive province, specific efforts were initiated by Shastri as police minister to deal with communal tensions in a proactive manner. He sought to ensure that the police force did not function in a manner that was biased towards any community. Living in a society that respected law and order and communal harmony was the right of all communities, and Shastri constantly underscored this point. Often, he himself would be present during tense situations and would advise the police to exercise restraint, even in the face of provocation. Over the years, communal flare-ups have often been the result of a partisan attitude and approach adopted by the police administration.

Rather than depoliticizing the functioning of the police, which Shastri sought to do, the police has increasingly become sensitive to political cues. This explains its inability to inspire confidence among the underprivileged sections of society and vulnerable social groups who look to the state for justice and protection.

Shastri brought into the upper cadres of the police, a large number of young people who had suffered imprisonment during the Quit India Movement. Those recruited were given sustained training to effectively orient them towards discipline and efficiency. Shastri's basic focus was to instil an element of humanism in the functioning of the police and to orient them to the fact of democracy. Fair play for him was paramount, even as effectiveness in maintaining law and order could not, in any way, be compromised. In all this, he led by example.

All those who had the opportunity to work with Shastri have been unequivocal in stressing the fact that he treated everyone who came to meet him with the same respect and dignity, irrespective of their social standing or economic status. This behaviour and attitude inspired those who worked with him, and they sought to follow suit in their interactions with the public. Over the years, recourse to the law-and-order machinery is seen as the first step to deal with citizens' protests and problems. When authorities are faced with public protests, the effort, as in Shastri's case, was to address the root of the problem. Today, more often than not, rather than addressing the cause of the problem, protests by the public are handled most insensitively as mere 'law and order' problems.

An interesting incident is reported during his tenure as the minister for police. On a visit to Agra, Shastri alighted from the train on reaching the station. As the train was early, the officers who were to welcome him had not yet arrived.

Shastri decided to walk towards the railway station entrance. He was stopped by a policeman who sternly told him that the minister for police was due to arrive and he should wait till the minister departed. At this moment, the officers who were to welcome him in the station arrived and pulled up the policeman for his behaviour. As the policeman was petrified at what he had done, Shastri calmed him down but asked him not to inconvenience common people by stopping them in anticipation of the arrival of a minister! One wonders where this approach has disappeared today. Privileges that flow from official positions are today seen as 'status symbols' and a 'right', not merely by the holders of the office but by the entire government machinery. Protecting this 'status' and flaunting 'privileges' have become the order of the day, placing the citizen to the greatest inconvenience.

Later, when Shastri was the HM at the national level, a similar incident occurred. He was on a visit to Calcutta (now Kolkata) and was caught in a traffic jam on the way to the airport. The CM asked the police to provide a lead vehicle with a siren to clear the way for the Union home minister. Shastri intervened and prevented this as he felt it would inconvenience the common people. He was fine with missing the flight but was totally against causing any disruption to the movement of traffic. Clearly, this is a stark contrast from what one notices nowadays. While the security threat today may be more visible and intense, and ministers need to have detailed security protocols and procedures, it may still be possible to ensure that people on the street are not inconvenienced on account of VIPs' movements. For Shastri, any display of power was a sign of arrogance, which, given a choice, he would never allow to be exercised.

As minister for police, he also constituted the Prantiya

Suraksha Sena, a semi-official civil defence unit in UP. It was a voluntary force that trained citizens for civil defence responsibilities at the time of emergencies or calamities. This initiative of Shastri was then also implemented in other states. As transport minister, he expanded the bus services in the province with a special focus on accessibility to rural areas. He developed a state-wide public transport network, which was both effective and efficient. Soon after Independence, he introduced an important innovation that had wider implications for social transformation and gender empowerment. In spite of the opposition from a few conservative sections, he got the transport department to recruit women bus conductors. Considered a step very few contemporaries would have been able to pull off, it was later hailed both for bringing in gender equality in the recruitment of bus conductors and for ensuring greater sensitivity in dealing with women passengers.

During his four years as a minister, Shastri's negotiation skills were on display in many a major crisis in the Congress party at the national level. In 1950, a contest for the post of party president became inevitable. This was one of the last major confrontations between Nehru and Vallabhbhai Patel. Soon, Jivatram Bhagwandas (J.B.) Kripalani and P.D. Tandon emerged as the rival candidates. While Kripalani had Nehru's blessings, Tandon was seen as Patel's candidate. In keeping with the Congress culture of consensus, the candidate for presidency was to be decided among the leadership by consensus. Patel believed that a consensus should have been arrived at on the choice of the Congress president, but Nehru decided to unilaterally announce Kripalani's name. This happened even as discussions were on to make Tandon the consensus candidate. Shastri was close to both Tandon and Nehru, and enjoyed the confidence of the two leaders. Tandon won the election, much to the unhappiness and discomfort of Nehru. Though Shastri did try to mediate, the tensions and differences went beyond the limits of manageability, resulting in Tandon's resignation and Nehru taking over as the Congress president.[30]

Important people influenced Shastri's life and approach in this vital phase. As mentioned earlier, Gandhi's influence was evident in his decision to leave school and plunge into the freedom movement. He would remain devoted to the principles espoused by Gandhi and practise them in his politics. Both Gandhi and Shastri were born on 2 October, though thirty-five years apart! Lala Lajpat Rai's writings and ideas also influenced his approach to public life. Bal Gangadhar Tilak's call for viewing politics and public life as a 'sacrifice' and not a 'privilege' was part of his core ideals. Dr Bhagwan Das was also a true inspiration to Shastri during his days at Kashi Vidyapeeth and shaped his views on humanism and the need for an integrated approach. The great teacher convinced his student that *'yeh baat bhi theek hai'* (this point is also right) was much more important than *'yeh baat hi theek hai'* (only this point is right). P.D. Tandon was a guide and mentor in the formative years, and encouraged him to take interest and get involved in civic affairs. Working with G.B. Pant in the UP administration was a great learning for Shastri. Above all, during this time, Shastri had got the chance to be groomed by Nehru and secure his trust and confidence.

This early phase of Shastri's political life, prior to his formal entry into national politics, has received very little attention, even in his many biographies. The focus has, more often than

[30]Shastri, S. (1991). Nehru And The Congress Party: The Nurturing Of A Nascent Democracy. *The Journal of Karnatak University: Social Sciences, 24,* pp. 67–76.

not, been on the period after his moving to the national capital, especially after succeeding Nehru as the PM. The reference to the early years of his public/political career has merely been a formal preliminary footnote or even a belated afterthought. However, this study would want to privilege this phase for multiple reasons:

- This phase of three decades, from the 1920s to the early '50s, represents a period that saw Shastri attempt to implement the core philosophy he believed in. The opportunities for public service, organizing the party, contesting elections and holding public office during this phase, all provided Shastri with that much-needed experience to test his principles, articulate his ideas and demonstrate his leadership skills. This testing of political waters was an important learning phase for Shastri.

- These years established the foundation for his long role in political/public life. Very few political leaders in this country have had the opportunity to work at multiple levels prior to rising to top positions. More often than not, they have straight been catapulted to top positions or have had the advantage of a family name to take them forward. It has often been found that leaders like Shastri, who had the advantage of observing and working in political parties and the government at multiple levels, brought a more realistic perspective to problem-solving and managing political and administrative challenges.

- This phase allowed the political leadership in the country to get acquainted with the success and positivity of the style of politics that was unique to

Shastri: his understanding of people's problems, his humane approach to citizens' issues grounded in his sensitivity, his humility and attention to detail, his practical outlook that focused on the solution and not the problem and, above all, the sense of consistency that one found in all that he said and did. A colleague underscored that Shastri was 'popular everywhere because you feel quite at home with him when you talk to him'. He had time for everyone who came to meet him.

- This stage saw Shastri set standards both for himself and for others. As the secretary of the party organization in a crucial election in the province, he was able to set the norms for the choice of candidates. As the first police and transport minister of the United Provinces after Independence, the innovations and reforms he introduced became a benchmark for his contemporaries as well as immediate successors.

- Shastri represented a style of leadership that did not believe in confrontation, but in taking all sections along. In this initial phase, he had no enemies and nobody disliked him, in spite of Shastri having differences of opinion with them. This skill requires an attitude of accommodation and transparent sincerity, both of which were abundantly in display in Shastri's dealings with people. An associate of Shastri rightly reflected that 'he [Shastri] is always anxious to be fair and very human. He always puts himself in the position of the suppliant in cases involving the administration... he treats every individual as an individual rather than part of the mass.'[31] Especially in the days after Independence, his home always welcomed guests, and whenever he was in town and at home, he would be busy meeting visitors individually, not collectively. Given the 'janata durbars' (public receptions) that leaders conduct and the media publicizes today, where the public are often made to feel that they are fortunate to get the opportunity for a brief audience with their chosen leader, Shastri's approach was refreshingly different. Each one who came to meet him was made to feel comfortable and given a patient hearing.

• Having grown up in Benaras, Shastri had the opportunity to relate to diversity in its many manifestations. L.P. Singh rightly points out that 'this city was also traditionally associated with a great deal of ritualism, sectarianism, religiosity... but one never saw any trace of these in Shastri.' Shastri was a 'healthy agnostic' and the influence of Dr Bhagwan Das was visible on him. The tilt towards humanism and spiritualism became the 'prism' for him to view religion. In the discharge of his public responsibilities as evidenced in the early years in the United Provinces, it is evident that he was 'free from obscurantist predilections (and)... could look at people and their problems with a breadth of vision unfettered by traditional notions of distinctions.'[32] On the different occasions that he was administered the oath of office, he took a solemn affirmation rather

[31]Hangen, W. "After Nehru, Who?" *Champion of Peace: Tribute to Shastri* by Sudarshan K. Savara, New Delhi: Gyan Mandir 1967, p. 101

[32]Singh, L.P. (1996). *Portrait of Lal Bahadur Shastri: A Quintessential Gandhian*. Ravi Dayal Publisher, p. 10–11

than take the oath in the name of God. Further, Shastri was firmly against all distinctions based on caste and creed. On an occasion when he saw a close associate treating Dalit invitees differently at a social gathering, Shastri refused to partake of food until everyone was treated in a similar manner. This strong commitment to treating everyone as equal in a society that is still marked by its strong hierarchies required both courage of conviction and the understanding of social reality. Shastri possessed both in abundance.

• One saw in Shastri what it meant to be a true leader of the masses. A master of compromise, who allowed each one to leave the table of dialogue with an important takeaway and a sense of dignity was the lasting image of him that all those who worked with him unanimously had. As a key party organizer at the city, district and provincial levels, who played an important role in making critical decisions involving the choice of candidates, policy priorities and reconciling factionalism, he ensured that his style created no enemies. His premium on generating a consensus, which became possible because of his inexhaustible patience and capacity to be empathetic to multiple viewpoints, was his biggest strength.

Shastri demonstrated that a bottom-up approach to politics allowed a learning experience that was invaluable. It involved climbing the ladder of power, step by step, stage by stage. In Shastri's case, each step had an important achievement and each stage provided valuable insights and learning. Being born in the United Provinces, where 'Indian politics is brewed and

Congress leaders are bred,[33] was an advantage for Shastri. A bottom-up approach in such a state, which was the epicentre of Indian politics then, had much greater value than a top-down approach that catapults people to the top and requires them to 'gaze down' and attempt to understand the ground reality. As compared to many of his contemporaries, this was his biggest strength and asset.

The political transitions in Shastri's life were often seamless and without any visible breaks. Every step forward seems to be a natural byproduct of a past event or development. Each new challenge he was assigned was due to his past record of success.

Shastri's early life and initial years of public service shaped his values and vision. His approach to politics and public life was anchored in this career-shaping phase. Once he moved to the national stage, the very 'grounded' and 'down to earth' sense of understanding people, policies and politics was his most prized asset, which had made his actions, approach and attitude distinctly different from other political leaders of his time. Hangen effectively captured the essence of these early years' experience when he said that Shastri is 'nearest to the mind and soil of India (as)… he reflects the strengths and weaknesses of the Indian villager.'[34]

---

[33]Brecher, M. (1966). *Succession in India: A Study in Decision-making*. Oxford University Press, p. 92

[34]Hangen, W. "After Nehru, Who?" *Champion of Peace: Tribute to Shastri* by Sudarshan K. Savara, New Delhi: Gyan Mandir 1967, p. 40

3

TO THE CENTRE STAGE

Having carved a niche for himself in the politics of the largest state of India, it was time for Lal Bahadur Shastri to move to the national capital—the nerve centre of political power. In the early years after Independence, moving to national politics was always considered a promotion and recognition by the party and the national leadership of one's political skills and capacities. Today, with the states emerging as the new centre of politics, many leaders would prefer to remain in state politics rather than move to the national stage, unless it is to occupy the top position!

This chapter deals with Shastri's role and responsibilities during a critical thirteen-year phase in national politics (1951–64). It commences with the preparation for the first general elections and ends with the death of PM Nehru. This is also the phase in which Shastri carves a unique space for himself in national politics. He assumed charge of a range of responsibilities in these years, each of which reflected the level of confidence the party and its leadership had in him. This phase marks a transition for Shastri from state to national politics, just two years before he reached the age of fifty!

As political parties were preparing for the first general elections of 1952, strategies were being worked out for how best to choose the candidates and campaign for securing people's support. In 1950, the politics over the election of the party president created a major crisis. J.B. Kripalani was pitted against P.D. Tandon. As mentioned previously, while Kripalani had the support of Nehru, Tandon was backed by Vallabhbhai Patel. This was both an ideological battle as well as a personal rivalry. Tandon represented the Far Right and had the strong support of Patel. Nehru opposed Tandon's right-wing stance. He saw Tandon's approach as symbolizing a 'revivalist outlook' and was critical of him for encouraging the very forces that were harmful to the interests of both the Congress party and the nation. In a bitterly fought contest, Nehru had threatened to resign as PM in the event of Tandon being elected. However, Tandon did emerge victorious. Nehru was furious and refused to join the CWC. He, of course, did not implement the threat to resign. In fact, soon after Tandon's election, Patel (in a lighter vein) is reported to have asked Rajagopalachari (who was playing the role of a mediator between Nehru and Patel) as to whether he had brought Jawaharlal's resignation![35]

However, Patel died soon after Tandon's election and the latter began facing multiple challenges in leading the party. His differences with Nehru only kept mounting and Nehru subsequently emerged as a near-unquestioned leader within the party. These differences were largely linked to the reservations that Nehru had about Tandon.

Shastri did try to play the role of a peacemaker between the two. The friction between Tandon and Nehru was very distressing for Shastri. In his own words, 'I came all the way from Lucknow to New Delhi to speak to Panditji. I had three meetings with him; one in the morning, the other in

---

[35]Shankar, V. (1974). *My Reminiscences of Sardar Patel* (Vol. 2). Macmillan Co. of India. p. 112

the afternoon, and the third at night. We had prolonged talks and I suggested to Panditji that some way should be found to avoid any further widening of the rift.[36] There was little hope of rapprochement and soon Tandon preferred to submit his resignation in the interests of the party and the nation. Tandon was succeeded by Nehru as party president.

Nehru was looking around for a leader who could discharge the responsibilities of the GS of the party and lead the organizational preparations for the 1952 general elections. While the discussion on different names for general secretaryship was on, Bidhan Chandra Roy, the CM of West Bengal, is believed to have suggested to Nehru the name of Shastri.[37] Nehru had been comfortable working with Shastri in the past and was aware of the skill set he possessed and the successes he had achieved. He was also witness to Shastri's capacities to resolve disputes and reconcile differences. In 1945, he had been appointed as GS in the United Provinces and was instrumental in ensuring the success of the Congress in the Provincial legislature elections in this large province. He had been largely responsible for bringing rivals to agree to candidates and helped launch a unified campaign. This experience would be useful when the nation prepared for its first post-Independence elections. Further, given his proximity to Tandon, it was felt that Shastri could help ensure a smooth transition and continuity. He had even tried to bring Tandon and Nehru closer, soon after Tandon was elected party president.

[36]Mankekar, D.R. (1965). *Lal Bahadur: A Political Biography*. Bombay: Popular Prakashan, pp. 91–2

[37]Rau, S.K. "Lal Bahadur: Will He Be Able to Deliver?" *Champion of Peace: Tribute to Shastri* by Sudarshan K. Savara, New Delhi: Gyan Mandir 1967, p. 59

It was with these factors in mind that Nehru, after consulting CM Pant, requested Shastri to resign as minister for home and transport in the United Provinces and move to Delhi as the 'All India General Secretary' of the Congress party. While Shastri accepted the offer, he is believed to have consulted Tandon, who also advised him to take on the new responsibility. While Shastri did not hide his proximity to Tandon, he always placed a premium on loyalty. After taking over as GS, he clearly discharged his responsibilities keeping in mind that Nehru was the party president and his loyalty to the leadership was total and transparent.

As party GS, Shastri was the nucleus of the whole process of drawing up candidates for the 1952 Lok Sabha elections. Nehru, in spite of being party president, could not devote too much time to party matters, as he had to pay full attention to his role as the PM. The responsibility thus, fell squarely on Shastri's shoulders. He toured the length and breadth of the country, meeting leaders at the provincial level and holding discussions on finalizing candidates for both the State Assembly and Lok Sabha elections.

His skills in settling factional differences and arriving at consensus candidates were truly put to test during this time. This was also the first election with universal adult franchise, and the party had to devise its electoral campaign in such a way as to garner support. It was no longer merely the party that won the country freedom. It had now to transform itself into a platform that sought people's support to govern the country.

Shastri's approach to the people and their problems was rooted in his honesty and discrete approach. This won him several friends and admirers over the years. His tenure as GS of the party prior to the first general election was one such phase. Veteran journalist Pran Chopra highlights Shastri's role as GS below[38]:

> The office of the General Secretary, as with most other offices in the Congress, does not have a clearly defined dimension. It swells and shrinks with the incumbent. Mr Shastri is not given by temperament to acquiring more of the reins of power than legitimately belong to the functions he is asked to perform. But in 1952, the office of General Secretary legitimately had very wide ranging functions and Mr Shastri did justice to them—quietly, discreetly, competently and, what is more important, honestly... Difficult personal and class conflicts have to be resolved so that the selection of suitable candidates would not be hampered. And when these conflicts could not be resolved, the High command had to send its representatives—which usually meant Mr Shastri as General Secretary—to intervene decisively.

The Congress won a resounding victory in the first-ever polls post Independence, in which every adult citizen had the right to vote. Shastri had now emerged as a leader whose name evoked instant recognition among party cadres across the country. He had developed a rapport with the CMs and state party presidents during the election campaign. They were all impressed by his unobtrusive style and his capacity to settle differences and bring together diverse viewpoints and perspectives. Mankekar avers that a great part of the credit for the 1952 victory should go to Shastri. Given Shastri's style, he preferred to allow Nehru to take the full credit for

---

[38]Chopra, P. "Shastri: A Man of Rich Experience." *Champion of Peace: Tribute to Shastri* by Sudarshan K. Savara, New Delhi: Gyan Mandir 1967, p. 23

the victory as both Congress president and India's PM.[39] This was an approach he had adopted earlier too, when he worked with Nehru in the Allahabad city unit of the Congress and the United Provinces Congress Committee. This self-effacing nature of Shastri was a characteristic that was visible at strategic political moments and will be pointed out as we move along.

PIONEERING ROLE AS RAILWAY AND TRANSPORT MINISTER

With the Congress victory in the 1952 general elections, a new Council of Ministers had to take office. Shastri had done an admirable job as GS of the party and played a crucial role in the success that it had achieved. Nehru felt that Shastri was now needed in the Cabinet and assigned him the key portfolio of railways and transport. Sustaining and expanding the road and rail transport network in India was crucial to India's development. Nehru had been very clear in his objectives when deciding who this portfolio should be allotted to. Given his responsibilities during the 1952 elections, Shastri himself had not contested and, thus, was not a member of the Lok Sabha. He was elected to the Rajya Sabha soon after his appointment as a Cabinet minister.

Commenting on the Nehru Cabinet, the editorial in *The Pioneer* on 15 May 1952 stated that the 'newcomers are not all dark horses because at least three of them—T.T. Krishnamachari, Lal Bahadur Shastri and V.V. Giri have considerable reputation already.'[40] On his entry into the Union Cabinet, Shastri brought with him the formidable stamp

---

[39]Mankekar, D.R. (1965). *Lal Bahadur: A Political Biography*. Bombay: Popular Prakashan, pp. 84–5

[40]From microfilms at NML.

of past achievements. He was clearly someone who drew attention with his actions and his understated presence. His silence at Cabinet meetings did not imply any disinterest in other subjects, but given his nature, he felt constrained to speak on matters relating to other ministers. Often, he would share his concerns privately with the PM and not bring it out openly in the Cabinet. Many view his silence as a reflection of his inability to communicate. His supporters saw it as a conscious desire to focus exclusively on responsibilities specifically assigned to him.

As railways and transport minister, Shastri had a clear focus. He wanted the railways and the transport network to play a pioneering role in facilitating the quick movement of both people and materials across the country. He also desired that the railways organization be people-centric and reorient its working to the requirements of Independent India. He also attempted to ensure that in the functioning of the railways, the voice of the different stakeholders was adequately heard. Whenever the occasion arose, he asked common people their views and suggestions to improve the efficiency of the railways. He kept in touch with members of the Parliament (MPs) from across political parties and sought their inputs on the reform and working of the railways. He also understood the importance of securing the confidence and support of the bureaucracy, and they were also appreciative of Shastri's style and approach.

Shastri focused attention on key users of the railways. He attempted to reduce the wide variation in services offered to Class I and Class III passengers. He abolished Class I and converted the former Class II into Class I. He started high-speed trains from the national capital to important cities and provided in them air-conditioned vestibules. He introduced air-conditioned chair-car compartments in trains covering short distances. He also paid special attention to improving the facilities provided to passengers travelling by Class III. The advanced reservation and sleeper facilities were started in this class. Fans were provided in these compartments and thali meals, which were available to passengers in other classes, were also made available to passengers in Class III.

Shastri paid considerable attention to improving the security of the railways as he realized that a lot of the pilferage in the railways was linked to internal challenges. A large quantum of the claims for compensation on booked consignments that were lost were on account of organized gang thefts. He got the railways to appoint a security adviser on the railway board. The railways also started the Watch & Ward Organization, which later went on to become the Railways Protection Force. He also increased the capacities of the Chittaranjan Locomotive Works for the production of engines. Shastri also planned to abolish Class III and have only the first and second classes, but could not implement this decision due to his resignation as railway minister in late 1956.

In the August of 1956, there was a major railway accident in Mahbubnagar, Andhra Pradesh,[41] killing as many as 112 people. Taking moral responsibility for the accident, Shastri tendered his resignation to the PM, but Nehru persuaded Shastri to withdraw his resignation. A few months later in November 1956, there was yet another railway accident in Ariyalur in Tamil Nadu. This tragedy resulted in 144 deaths. Shastri promptly submitted his resignation to the PM and pleaded for its early acceptance.

This second resignation offered by Shastri attracted nation-

---

[41]Mahbubnagar now falls in the state of Telangana.

wide attention. *The Pioneer* in its editorial on 26 November 1956, soon after the Ariyalur accident, said that 'accidents happen in the best regulated railways, but then accidents ought to be exceptions rather than the rule.'[42] While making out a case for greater safety measures, it did not hold the railway minister responsible in any way. In his resignation letter, Shastri felt that 'it will be good for me and the Government as a whole, if I quietly quit the office I hold.'[43] It may be important to underscore the use of the word 'quietly' by Shastri, as this appeared to be his second nature.

Nehru summed up the dilemma he faced when he conceded in the Lok Sabha that it was a difficult decision for him. He went on to say that he had the highest regard for Shastri and 'from the broader point of view of constitutional propriety that we should set an example in this and no man should think that whatever might happen, we carry on without being affected by it.'[44] Nehru hinted that if he did accept the resignation, it would be on the grounds of constitutional propriety. This needs to be highlighted, as justifying the acceptance of the resignation on this principle became the object of severe criticism in the media.

THE RESIGNATION THAT SET THE GOLD STANDARD

When it appeared that Nehru seemed inclined to accept the resignation, thirty MPs appealed to Nehru not to let Shastri go. They were of the view that while Shastri should be lauded for having offered to resign, his resignation should not be accepted, as he was not personally responsible for

---

[42]From microfilms at NML.
[43]From microfilms at NML.
[44]Lok Sabha Speech. *The Pioneer*. (1956, November 26). Microfilms at NML.

the accident. The mishap was on account of technical failure for which the railways board should take responsibility. The parliamentarians were clear that the bureaucracy should take the blame and not the political executive.

However, Shastri did have his way and Nehru forwarded the resignation to the president for acceptance. Speaking in the Lok Sabha on the matter, Nehru elaborated[45]:

> On receipt of this letter, I talked to him also last night when I saw the great distress of his mind and the burden he was carrying. Afterwards I thought of it again and I came to the conclusion that it would be better for me [to advise]... the President to accept his resignation, not because I hold the Railway Minister responsible—obviously not—and I have also spoken in high terms of his work and joint work we have done together... no man can wish for a better colleague in any undertaking... A man of the highest integrity, loyalty, devoted to the ideal, a man of conscience and a man of hard work. We can expect no better. It is because he is such a man of conscience that he [feels] deeply whenever there is any failing in the responsibility entrusted to his charge.

In this speech, Nehru makes no reference to constitutional propriety. He hailed Shastri as a valued colleague and a man of conscience, integrity and total loyalty. The 'constitutional propriety' reference he made in his first intervention on the issues was the focus of the media. *The Pioneer* came down heavily on the PM for having accepted Shastri's resignation. In its editorial of 28 November 1956, while making a distinction between self-immolation and hara-kiri in strong words,

---

[45]Lok Sabha Speech. *The Pioneer*. (1956, November 26). Microfilms at NML.

it stated that Nehru's conduct in making a martyr out of an 'exceptionally conscientious and hardworking colleague [was] wholly unwarranted'. The editorial further said it did not see any point in first making someone a superman and then throwing him out, citing some non-existent 'constitutional propriety'. The editorial also argued that, in reality, one needs to focus on what is 'feasible' rather than 'desirable'.

Yet, over the years, Shastri's decision to quit, owning moral responsibility for the train disaster, has been frequently quoted to remind ministers of their ethical obligations. Very few have followed Shastri's example, and even when they have, it has been more of a mask to cover blatantly personal or political goals.

By his actions, Shastri seemed to have set a high benchmark. It may not have been followed by others, but it became an important barometer to measure Shastri's own political credentials and credibility. The fact that even six decades after the incident, it is regarded as the gold standard on/for ethical norms and probity goes to indicate how the decision to resign is assessed. Beyond doubt, it placed Shastri on a pedestal.

GEARING UP FOR THE GENERAL ELECTIONS

Though Nehru had accepted the resignation of Shastri, he had hinted on a future course of action in his first intervention on this matter in the Lok Sabha. He went on to add that Shastri would continue to be associated with the party in the future too. It could be argued that Nehru persuaded himself to accept Shastri's resignation, as he felt it would help him assign work to Shastri relating to the party. Soon after Shastri's resignation was accepted, he was designated by Nehru as the chief organizer for the Congress party campaign in the 1957 general elections. Shastri would have to perform a role similar to what he had done in the 1952 elections.

Shastri played a crucial role in the choice of party candidates and devising the campaign strategy. By then, factionalism in the party had become clearly evident. Shastri consciously distanced himself from all factions and, in the process, won the support of all groups. Pran Chopra highlights Shastri's role in this regard[46]:

> Mr Shastri, with one leg in the camp of the old guard, was thus able to place the other leg in the new camp. The part he played, with the full backing of the Prime Minster, gave him a unique say in the choice of Congress candidates in these elections and therefore made him a person whom the rival wings of the Congress in all the states wanted to impress with their respective virtues.

This time around, Shastri contested the Lok Sabha elections from Allahabad. Not only did he register a confident victory, he also ensured that the party did well and returned to power, securing the people's mandate. His organizational skills were instrumental in helping the party put up a creditable performance in the first two general elections of Independent India.

Two eminent journalists refer to Shastri's resignation and his being assigned a role in the Congress organization as being closely linked. Louis Kraar, the chief of bureau in *The Times*, New Delhi, wrote, 'Shastri knew that Nehru needed him to run the party's next election campaign... In retrospect

---

[46]Chopra, P. "Shastri: A Man of Rich Experience." *Champion of Peace: Tribute to Shastri* by Sudarshan K. Savara, New Delhi: Gyan Mandir 1967, p. 25

his dramatic resignation was mostly a clever political ploy.'[47] Pran Chopra chooses a slightly different route of explanation. While recognizing that the act of resignation was unselfish, Chopra asserts that 'this action secured him [Shastri] a double advantage. It focused the country's attention upon him more than ever before, and since it had relieved him of Government duties, it freed him for the biggest political assignment to date.'[48]

With the Congress party returning to power in the 1957 elections, Nehru had to once again constitute his Council of Ministers. Less than five months after resigning as railway minister, Shastri was back in the Union Cabinet in April 1957, as the minister for transport and communications. Years later, H.R. Vohra, when writing in *The Guardian*, commented that Shastri 'was never the type to run after political office but invariably found himself in it.'[49] His tenure in this ministry was for less than a year. In this period, he initiated the process of starting the Vishakhapatnam Shipyard and also amicably resolved a strike of the Post and Telegraph employees.

MORE RESPONSIBILITIES, MORE TROUBLESHOOTING MISSIONS

In the March of 1958, when T.T. Krishnamachari resigned as finance minister, Morarji replaced him. Shastri was asked to take over Morarji's portfolio of industry and commerce.

---

[47]Kraar, L. "India's New Chief—The Softness of Silk and Hardness of Steel." *A Study of Lal Bahadur Shastri*, B.S. Gujarati, Delhi: Sterling, 1965, p. 71

[48]Chopra, P. "Shastri: A Man of Rich Experience." *Champion of Peace: Tribute to Shastri* by Sudarshan K. Savara, New Delhi: Gyan Mandir 1967, p. 24.

[49]From microfilms at NML.

Given Shastri's strong commitment to socialism, his role and performance in this ministry were carefully watched. This ministry has also been a test of the integrity of the minister assigned with the portfolio. In his actions during the three years that he managed these departments, there was not even a whiff of a controversy that pointed to any unethical practice. C.P. Srivastava highlights that this record of integrity gave a further boost to his stature and reputation.

Many years later in 1965, Shastri elaborated on his attitude towards business. This, clearly, was his approach even when he was the industry minister. He felt businessmen had an 'even greater role than that of an economist and the politician. Too often, the community views the businessman's aim as selfish gain... [That] impression can be removed only when [a] business becomes fully alive to its social responsibilities.'[50]

During his tenure as industry minister, he focused on strengthening the public sector in the heavy industries segment. Shastri additionally focused attention on the agro industry. Mankekar underscores the fact that bringing together agriculture and industry was critical to resolving the unemployment challenges in rural India. A record 14–15 per cent industrial output was evidenced in 1960, which far exceeded the Plan targets. There was a significant increase in the number of applications from all over the country for starting new enterprises. This was reflective of the congenial environment that had been built up to encourage private initiative and investment.

Thus, over a four-year span (1957–61), Shastri looked after the responsibilities of the crucial portfolios of transport,

---

[50] *The Times of India.* (1965, March 16). Speech while inaugurating a seminar on Social Responsibility of Business.

communications, industry and commerce, and demonstrated that diligence, commitment and hard work were critical to success. He spent long hours at the ministry and came back home late in the night. This did create anxieties in his family about his health. PM Nehru often advised him to return home early. He would follow it for a few days and then get back to his routine of staying up late into the night at the office. This eventually took a toll on his health and he suffered his first heart attack in October 1958, while on a visit to Allahabad. He recovered quickly and was back to a gruelling work schedule.

His desire to give a patient hearing to all those who came to meet him often led to long interactions. He would hardly heed the advice of his assistants to cut short a discussion as he felt he needed to give due attention to those who had come all the way to seek his audience. Even at formal meetings, he would encourage everyone to speak, express their frank opinions and then arrive at a decision after taking into account all the inputs offered. Commenting on this approach, L.P. Singh, who had an opportunity to observe Shastri closely, felt that Shastri did not have a strict timetable to solve problems. This gave him the necessary flexibility to allow each group to express itself and give time and space for a solution acceptable to all parties to emerge. While this style and approach made each one feel that their voice was given due respect, it required Shastri to spend long hours in deliberations and discussions.[51]

In February 1961, HM G.B. Pant fell seriously ill and PM Nehru asked Shastri to additionally take charge of the home portfolio. This was indicative of the trust that Nehru placed in Shastri. Traditionally (even today) the portfolio of

---

[51]Singh, L.P. (1996). *Portrait of Lal Bahadur Shastri: A Quintessential Gandhian*. Ravi Dayal Publisher, p. 30.

home affairs is often assigned to the minister immediately after the PM.

In April 1961, when Pant passed way, there was an intense debate in the corridors of power on who would be made the HM. Some thought that this would also determine the line of succession after Nehru. Morarji, who was then the finance minister, was a strong contender. But Nehru decided to make Shastri the HM. In his memoirs, Morarji provides his version of why Shastri pipped him to the post.[52] Morarji opines that Nehru 'was afraid that if the Home Ministry was entrusted to me, it would increase my political importance a great deal. Ultimately, it was entrusted to Shri Lal Bahadur Shastri, who always carried out Jawaharlalji's wishes and did not do anything which he did not like.'

The question also arose as to who should be the deputy leader of the party in the Lok Sabha. Morarji was keen on the position, but there was stiff opposition from his other Cabinet colleagues. Shastri was asked to work out a solution by Nehru. When Shastri found that there was no unanimity on the choice of the deputy leader, he came up with an alternative. He suggested that there should be two deputy leaders, one for the Lok Sabha and one for the Rajya Sabha. He also proposed that they should be members of the House but not ministers. This proposal was welcomed and implemented. Morarji himself was not happy with the suggestion but had no choice but to accept it.[53]

In some ways, entrusting the MHA to Shastri was the first indication given by PM Nehru of his choice of successor. As Morarji himself concedes—not transferring him from finance

---

[52]Desai, M. (1979). *The Story of My Life*. Bombay: Pergamon
[53]Choudary, P. & Shastri, A. (2015). *Lal Bahadur Shastri: Lessons in Leadership*, Delhi: Wisdom Village Publications, pp. 77–8

to home was a sign of Nehru wanting to limit Morarji's political stature. It could also be a reflection of the faith that Nehru had in Shastri's ability to handle sensitive issues that the HM was required to deal with, and Shastri was sent on many troubleshooting missions as the HM. For political leaders, loyalty is often the most important quality they look for when entrusting colleagues with sensitive tasks. Clearly, Shastri fitted the requirement perfectly. An added bonus was his skill set and competence in undertaking a task with diligence and efficiency. His qualities and capacities as reflected in his work were the best credentials.

Commenting on the sharp contrast between Shastri and his predecessor in the MHA, G.B. Pant, often referred to as the 'Tiger of Kumaon', Welles Hangen elaborates[54]:

> Watching Shastri enter the high-domed chamber of the Lok Sabha for the first time after Pant's time, I was struck by the contrast. Shastri seemed almost furtive as he slipped unnoticed on the Government front bench. Pant's entrances always sent a stir through the huge hall. The contrast was even more marked when Shastri rose to speak in a small monotone. His words were lost in the hubbub of heedless legislators. Pant, on the other hand, always held Parliament spellbound. I soon realized that he (Shastri) was neither overwhelmed not overawed by the immense responsibilities that had been thrust on him... his rare humility and genuine compassion set him apart.

Veteran journalist Kuldip Nayar has also commented on the

---

[54]Hangen, W. "After Nehru, Who?" Champion of Peace: Tribute to Shastri by Sudarshan K. Savara, New Delhi: Gyan Mandir 1967, p. 98

contrasting personalities of Pant and Shastri.[55] He was more comfortable working with Shastri on account of his simple nature and Shastri's capacity to make people feel relaxed in his presence. While both Pant and Shastri had their unique positive qualities, they represented contrasting styles and Shastri brought to the MHA the stamp of his unique approach.

AS HOME MINISTER: KINGPIN OF THE WHOLE CENTRAL MACHINERY

There are several major developments that merit attention while assessing Shastri's tenure as HM. Each development was riddled with multiple complications and required tact, patience and negotiation skills to move towards a resolution. Each of these developments had important long-term implications. A review of the performance of successive HMs in India has indicated that their ability to manage sensitive political issues relating to the states of India has played a major role in measuring the degree of success they achieved as HMs. Highlighting Shastri's approach, L.P. Singh believes that 'with all its power and panoply—there was the soul of a servant of the people, tempered through years of dedicated social service.'[56]

Even before Shastri formally took charge as HM, there was a simmering controversy brewing in Assam. It required his immediate intervention soon after he took over the home portfolio. The state had a majority Assamese-speaking population but a sizeable Bengali-speaking population too. For

[55]Nayar, K. (2012). *Beyond the Lines: An Autobiography*. Roli Books Private Limited, p. 131

[56]Singh, L.P. (1996). *Portrait of Lal Bahadur Shastri: A Quintessential Gandhian*. Ravi Dayal Publisher, p. 113

official purposes, Assamese, Bengali and English were all used. In 1959, the Assam Sahitya Sabha demanded that Assamese be formally pronounced as the official language of the state. A direct corollary of this development was a campaign against the Bengalis. Sporadic language riots broke out in different parts of the state, resulting in both violence and casualties. In October 1960, the State Assembly passed the Assam Official Language Act, which made Assamese the official language of the state. In the Cachar district of Assam, which saw a heavy concentration of the Bengali-speaking population, there was a massive protest and the demand for Bengali being declared as an additional official language. In the May of 1961, language riots erupted once again, causing tension in the region.

As the HM, Shastri decided to visit Assam and discuss the problem with the government authorities as well as the contending groups. He gave a patient hearing to all the parties to the dispute and convinced them to repose confidence in his impartiality and fairness. On reviewing the issue, Shastri realized that a compromise formula needed to be worked out. The States Reorganisation Commission had earlier proposed that if more than 70 per cent of the people in a state spoke a single language, the state could be declared unilingual. If the majority language-speaking group constituted less than 70 per cent, then the state should favour a bilingual or multilingual policy, as the case may be. As per the 1951 census, the proportion of the Assamese-speaking people was less than 70 per cent. Shastri then came up with a proposal, which became popular as the 'Shastri formula'. This was acceptable to all the parties involved in the dispute.

The Shastri formula basically provided for the use of three languages—Assamese, Bengali and English—in the Cachar district of Assam. Correspondence between the Cachar district administration and the Assam government could be undertaken in any of these three languages. In the Cachar district office and in educational institutions, both Assamese and Bengali could be used. Given the Bengali-speaking majority in the district, their language got precedence in the district. It required Shastri's persuasive skills to get all parties to agree to the formula, resulting in the resolution of the dispute. The earnestness of his intentions and the fair manner in which he heard out all the parties were major factors in his gaining their confidence. Later in the 1980s, when Assam was on the boil again, it was clear that the central leadership could not resolve the problem in the early stages and did not possess the persuasive skills that Shastri had displayed.

Even today, the debate on the proposed Citizenship Act in the Northeast has become the focus of alarming divisiveness, simply because the leadership has not been able to gain the confidence of all the groups. The earnestness of intentions, which was the true hallmark of Shastri's style, seems to have become a rarity in today's efforts at problem-solving. An approach of inclusiveness marked Shastri's style and approach, something that is sadly missing in modern-day leaders, save for the catchy slogans they espouse.

An interesting episode linked to the solving of the crisis in Assam is often referred to. When Shastri was driving down to Silchar, the district headquarters of Cachar, young boys and girls lined up on both sides of the road with placards in their hands, participating in a silent protest. On reaching Silchar, Shastri first went to the hospital to meet those who had been wounded in the police action. He next went to the jail to talk to those who had been imprisoned for taking part in the agitation. He then spoke to the family members of those killed, and offered his condolences. He finally landed up at the Circuit House late at night. The leaders of the agitating movement had been waiting here for him for a long time. Shastri spoke to each one of them and at the end, the feeling of bitterness, rivalry and ill will had been diluted. It was now much easier to resolve the crisis. By attending to the victims first and protestors next, Shastri had sent out an important message on who needed to be prioritized.

A second issue that Shastri was required to resolve as HM was the crisis in Punjab, caused by the agitation launched by Master Tara Singh of the Akali Dal. In August 1961, Singh intensified an agitation for the creation of a 'Punjabi Suba', contending that the Sikhs have been unfairly treated by the central government. Shastri appointed a three-member Commission of Inquiry to study the situation and make its recommendations. In its recommendations, the commission stated that there was no discrimination against the Sikhs in Punjab. It concluded that Sikhs 'in and outside Punjab are an honoured part of Indian society.' The agitation subsided. Shastri had handled the challenge with great finesse, involving both a degree of conciliation and firmness of resolve.

As HM, Shastri also had to deal with the increasing sentiment in the Madras state (now Chennai) that North India was seeking to dominate over the South. On a visit to the state, he held discussions with leaders of the Dravida Munnetra Kazhagam (DMK) to assure them that the North had no such intentions of seeking to dictate terms to the South of India. On his return to Delhi, he ensured that legislation was put in place that if political parties or individuals were to speak of secession, it would be a penal offence. This resulted in the DMK having to amend the constitution to survive as a political party.

Shastri built an excellent rapport with the CMs of

various states and they all respected him for his principles and conduct. An interesting episode that occurred in 1962 merits attention. It relates to the coalition government in Kerala headed by Thanu Pillai, a veteran politician whose role in politics preceded independence in the United State of Travancore and Cochin[57]. There was a minor crisis brewing in Kerala. The state had a coalition government involving the PSP and the Congress. Though PSP was the junior partner, its leader, Pillai, headed the coalition. The Congress party, which was the senior partner, was unhappy with the way the CM was functioning.

To resolve the differences between the CM and his Congress colleagues, Shastri came down to Trivandrum (now Thiruvananthapuram) and held wide-ranging discussions with the senior bureaucracy, Congress leaders and the CM. Shastri attempted to place before Pillai the grievances of the Congress leaders. Pillai replied that while he agreed with the reasonableness of Shastri's suggestion, he was unable to change his style in view of his long-established political standing. He went on to tell Shastri that he has been a patriot all his life and would be happy to serve the country in any other capacity. After consulting some more people, Shastri got Pillai appointed as the governor of Punjab.

However, the PSP was upset with Shastri for having forced Pillai to resign and accept the governorship. In the light of Pillai's silence, Shastri too decided not to elaborate on the reasons for making him a governor. He felt that he would betray the confidence that Pillai had vested in him and did not think it right to expose a colleague to protect his own image. Over the years, in his dealings with colleagues, Shastri ensured

---

[57]These two princely states are now a part of the state of Kerala.

that his actions and stand evoked trust among them, and the Thanu Pillai incident is a case in point.

The above incident of a smaller coalition partner (PSP) facing difficulties with the larger coalition partner (Congress) indicates how tact, patience and trust, which Shastri employed, are needed to resolve such delicate issues. Such developments have become quite common in the states today. More often than not, crises and differences in the coalitions result in their collapse, as the leadership is not proactive in averting or resolving them. Shastri's approach, attitude and actions in the early '60s are relevant for political leaders even today.

Shastri was also tasked with resolving the highly emotive question of the official language of the Union. Article 341 of the Constitution established Hindi as the official language of the Union with effect from January 1965. The states of South India were keen that as per the provisions of Article 341 (3) (a), an indefinite extension be provided for the continued use of English. While speaking at the All India Youth Conference at Tirupati in September 1962, Shastri made his stand clear on the language issue. He said that unless Hindi could be sufficiently developed and the people learnt it well, he didn't see any point in imposing it. He also said that he would prefer to make English the common language since it was spoken in all the states. Shastri's stand, as enunciated in his Tirupati speech, became the basis of the Official Languages Act of 1963 (OLA). As HM, Shastri piloted this measure and got the Parliament to approve of the same.

The friction on the language issue, which has continued to surface from time to time, is often linked to the insensitivity demonstrated by the Hindi-speaking states and people to the genuine concerns of those regions of India where Hindi is not the mother tongue. People accept Hindi when allowed to do so at their pace and conviction. But when attempts are made to force people to communicate in or accept Hindi, it often creates an emotional backlash. It needs to be recognized that the anti-Hindi agitation that emerged in many parts of South India was not so much against the language per se, but was a revolt against the domination that the language came to represent. Shastri, hailing from the Hindi heartland himself, was able to convince people in the non-Hindi speaking states, of the earnestness of his intentions. This was something to which even some of his Cabinet colleagues were not sensitive. D.R. Mankekar succinctly emphasizes that Shastri 'won the confidence of the South by his ready recognition of the Southerners' genuine difficulty in agreeing to the displacement of English in favour of Hindi as the medium of official communication in the Central Government.'[58] In the recent past, this approach has unfortunately not been taken by many political leaders from the Hindi heartland and has been the root cause of continued tensions on the language issue.

Another issue that required Shastri's attention was managing the implementation of the Emergency at the time of the Chinese aggression of 1962. Shastri closely monitored internal security developments and ensured that the powers vested in the government during the Emergency were not misused. He took keen interest in the actions of his ministry to coordinate with other agencies in the defence of the country. Shastri had always been suspicious of the Chinese and their intentions, and was persuaded by Sardar Patel's stance on China. Shastri was convinced that China was trying to hoodwink India by making a show of its peaceful intentions.

---

[58]Mankekar, D.R. (1965). *Lal Bahadur: A Political Biography*. Bombay: Popular Prakashan, p. 97

He also had serious differences with Defence Minister V.K. Krishna Menon and felt that he had misguided the PM on India's defence preparedness. On Shastri's visits to the border areas, he found that the reports from the ground did not conform to the inputs that were being provided to the defence minister, and whenever possible, brought this to the PM's attention. Finally, Nehru's decision to move Krishna Menon from defence to defence production, and finally being eased out of the Cabinet, did see Shastri playing an important role. In fact, in 1962, when Shastri's advice was sought by Nehru on the formation of the Cabinet, Shastri had suggested the defence production portfolio against Menon's name. While Nehru did not accept Shastri's suggestion, it became a reality two years later. The dislike was mutual. Menon was aware of Shastri's role in advising Nehru to drop him from the Cabinet and, later, was a key player supporting Morarji in the prime ministerial race.

Shastri was also keen to address as HM the rising spiral of corruption in the administration. The Central Bureau of Investigation (CBI) was set up in February 1963. Shastri was keen that this bureau functions with an element of autonomy and not be seen as yet another agency of the government. Given its mandate to investigate cases involving the violation of norms and rules, he was a strong advocate of it being allowed to function independently, even as it remained accountable in its approach and methods.

An interesting episode is often quoted in this regard. It is closely linked to Shastri's approach and attitude towards corruption and corrupt practices. As the HM, he was privy to a CBI report that indicated that a minister in the government, Keshav Dev Malaviya, was a beneficiary in a financial transaction involving a mineral lessee. He felt it was his immediate responsibility to bring this to the attention of the

PM. An inquiry by a judge of the Supreme Court was ordered, which found the minister guilty, resulting in his resignation. Malaviya had been a close friend of Shastri's, so the latter decided to meet Malaviya at his residence to express his sympathy. On reaching Malaviya's residence, Shastri was confronted by Malaviya's wife, who used strong language against him and condemned what she termed as his hypocrisy. Shastri withdrew and returned to his office, deeply hurt by the encounter. L.P. Singh, who was present in the office when Shastri returned, says that the HM 'recognized that giving in to personal sympathy for the victim of one's official action, combined with a reputation for avoiding giving offence, could have very disagreeable consequences.'[59]

A code of conduct for ministers was laid down during Shastri's tenure in the MHA. He was also instrumental in the constitution of the Santhanam Committee, which was tasked with the responsibility of examining corruption at both the political and administrative levels[60] and suggest remedies to tackle the same. Many of the committee's recommendations were later implemented when Shastri became the PM.

As HM, Shastri was also tasked with his first mission outside India. Tensions between Nepal and India had reached an alarming level by the March of 1963. There was a growing perception in the Indian establishment that Nepal was veering closer to both China and Pakistan and distancing itself from India. PM Nehru decided to put Shastri's negotiation skills to test in dealing with an important and sensitive neighbour. Shastri embarked on his first foreign trip and landed in Kathmandu. Even as Shastri arrived, the political atmosphere

---

[59]Singh, L.P. (1996). *Portrait of Lal Bahadur Shastri: A Quintessential Gandhian*. Ravi Dayal Publisher, pp. 23–4
[60]Ibid

appeared tense and the media carried strong anti-India reports and statements by leaders.

Shastri had several rounds of meetings with King Mahendra and also held wide-ranging discussions with the chairman of the Council of Ministers and the HM. His principal objective was to dispel the fear that India was bent on behaving like a 'big brother'. He convinced his Nepali counterparts that India had no intention of interfering in the internal affairs of its neighbours. The tension in the relations between the countries appeared to have reduced and the joint communiqué issued at the end of the visit reflected this improved understanding in both countries of each other's perspectives. While responding to a specific question at a press conference on Nepal being close to China, Shastri disarmed the journalists by saying, 'It is entirely for Nepal to decide its policy and course of action.' Shastri clearly won the hearts of the Nepali leadership and his first diplomatic foray was considered a singular success.

Finally, there was an important task that Shastri initiated as HM, though it could not be taken to its logical conclusion during his tenure in the ministry. He was very eager to revamp the administration and initiate major reforms. Inspired by the success of the Hoover Commission in the US, Shastri was keen to appoint a similar high-power commission to review the working of the administration and suggest reforms. The reforms framework that Shastri envisaged involved multiple levels and processes. He was keen to find a solution to the inordinate delays in decision-making. The district-level administration has been the nucleus of implementing development and welfare-related policies as well as ensuring law and order; Shastri favoured a searching second look at the district administration. The state and central administration and the organization of the secretariat at these two levels were also top priorities.

Transforming the attitude and approach of the civil service was also a prime focus, as was developing healthy norms to govern the minister–civil servant relationship. This earnest desire became a reality when he became PM. Morarji chaired this committee and it was later presided over by Kengal Hanumanthaiah when Morarji joined Indira Gandhi's Cabinet. The first Administrative Reforms Commission report was submitted during Indira Gandhi's prime ministership. While a few key recommendations were implemented, the government lacked the political will to take the reform proposals to their logical conclusions. A member of the commission, H.V. Kamath, in a discussion with me, more than four decades ago, had said that the bureaucracy succeeded in scuttling the reforms proposals as their implementation would have limited the power and influence that the civil service had come to exercise in the administration.

The best compliment to Shastri as HM appeared in the editorial of a leading newspaper, which said that the 'kingpin of the whole central machinery is, of course, the Home Minister, Lal Bahadur Shastri, who can predict Mr Nehru's views with rare clarity.'[61]

KAMARAJ PLAN: TOWARDS GEOGRAPHICAL EQUITY AND IDEOLOGICAL BALANCE

With the Congress being in power for sixteen years at a stretch (1947–63), there was a growing feeling that important leaders of the party were more actively involved in the government

---

[61]Hangen, W. "After Nehru, Who?" *Champion of Peace: Tribute to Shastri* by Sudarshan K. Savara, New Delhi: Gyan Mandir 1967, p. 39

rather than in strengthening the party. The view was also repeatedly heard in several important quarters that the gulf between the party and the government was widening with every passing day. The war with China had also taken its toll on the image of both the party and the leadership. The Congress party suffered a string of defeats in by-elections held in May 1963. Three leaders who had now emerged as key opponents of PM Nehru—J.B. Kripalani, Ram Manohar Lohia and Minoo Masani—emerged victorious in these by-elections.

It is in this context that the CM of the Madras state, K. Kamaraj, came up with a proposal (which later became famous as the Kamaraj Plan) that senior ministers both at the national and state levels should resign from the government and work for the party organization. This would also give an opportunity to infuse fresh blood into the ministry. This proposal was placed before the All India Congress Committee session in August 1963 and unanimously approved. It was given the final consent by the CWC. In his note to the CWC, PM Nehru said that 'the top personalities in the Congress who are now in high office should retire and devote themselves to organizational and other forms of service to the people.'

Even as the proposal was being discussed, there were diverse reactions in the media, ranging from cautious optimism to outright criticism. *The Statesman* in its editorial hinted that the plan may have two virtues—boldness and simplicity—but it could be dangerous in the long run. On 14 August 1963, S. Mulgaonkar, a respected editor, opined in *Hindustan Times* that the plan might not necessarily have addressed the deeper malady of the wide gulf between the Congress and the people.[62] In the same paper on the same day, Kasturiranga

---

[62]From microfilms at NML.

Santhanam was also of the view that this plan was a mere first step in a 'movement for national purification'. Thus, while it was appreciated in a muted manner, the feeling was that much more needed to be done.

As part of the Kamaraj Plan, six Union ministers and six CMs resigned. Jagjivan Ram (Transport and Communications), Morarji Desai (Finance), Lal Bahadur Shastri (Home), Sadashiv Kanoji Patil (Food and Agriculture) Bezawada Gopala Reddy (Information and Broadcasting) and Kalu Lal Shrimali (Education) were the Union ministers who quit the Cabinet. K. Kamaraj (Madras), Chandra Bhanu Gupta (UP), Binodanand Jha (Bihar), Biju Patnaik (Orissa [now Odisha]), Bakshi Ghulam Mohammad (Jammu and Kashmir [J&K]) and Bhagwantrao Mandloi (Madhya Pradesh) were the CMs who resigned. Michael Brecher observed that the Kamaraj Plan provided for both 'geographical equity' and 'ideological balance'.

It has been stated in some quarters that Nehru was not keen to let Shastri leave the Cabinet as part of the Kamaraj Plan. However, Shastri persuaded Nehru to allow him to do so. Nehru agreed to Shastri's resignation, as he did not want to appear playing favourites. It is also asserted that the Kamaraj Plan was essentially aimed at easing out Morarji from the government. The fact that, save Shastri, none of the other Union ministers who resigned were specifically assigned any organizational work in the party, lends credence to this view.

The media too pointed out the lack of any meaningful reform that the Kamaraj Plan would produce. *The Hindu*, in its editorial, spoke of the need for the 're-examining of policies rather than for a mere reshuffling of personalities.'[63] Renowned commentator Kishan Bhatia felt that the Kamaraj Plan may

---

[63]From microfilms at NML.

have 'only shifted the venue of the leaders' internal struggle for supremacy from the Cabinet room to the Congress office.'[64] Drawing a comparison between Shastri's resignation as railway minister and under the Kamaraj Plan, *The Statesman* said, tongue in cheek, that 'this time the accident seems calculated with calculations remaining obscure.'[65] The general discontent with the direction in which the government was moving was apparent.

Reflecting on the political compulsions that necessitated the inclusion of Shastri's Kamaraj Plan, Brecher believes that it was an act of political balancing and left the debate on his political successor to be fought in the public domain. Shastri himself reflected on his leaving the Cabinet in a letter he wrote to a friend soon after these developments. He said[66]:

> I have always been feeling uncomfortable in my mind about giving advice to others and not acting upon it myself. The speed with which we in the Congress are going down is something frightening... No strong opposition party has been able to emerge. In these circumstances, if some of us in Government come out and do something then this relinquishing of office should be welcomed.

SYNDICATE FIRST

On resigning from the Cabinet, Shastri was appointed as a member of the Parliamentary Board and Organisational

---

[64]Bhatia, K. (1963, September 1). *The Hindu*. From microfilms at MNL.

[65]*The Statesman*. (1963, August 30). From microfilms at NML.

[66]Letter to Rajeshwar Prasad, dated 6 October 1963, quoted in *Lal Bahadur Shastri: An Illustrated Biography*, Mithrapuram K. Alexander; New Delhi: New Light Publications, 1967, p. 32

Committee. This required him to travel the length and breadth of the country to meet party leaders and workers. Soon after the implementation of the Kamaraj Plan, the choosing of a president for the Congress became the focus of the party's attention. Neelam Sanjiva Reddy, the CM of Andhra Pradesh, felt that the election for party president was like Stage 2 of the Kamaraj Plan. It has also been asserted that in the internal dynamics of the Congress party, a Syndicate had emerged.[67] Though the Syndicate was formed during Nehru's time, it only came into prominence in the post-Nehruvian years.

There was a near consensus with the Congress leadership that the choice of the new president of the party should be unanimous. The Syndicate first thought of Shastri for this post. If they did not receive a positive response from him, they would fall back on Kamaraj. The aim was to keep Morarji out of the reckoning. As the discussion continued, it became clear that if Shastri's name was to be proposed, Morarji would enter the fray and force a contest. Shastri too was reluctant to offer his name for the presidency. Brecher highlights three factors that held Shastri back. Firstly, he may have been biding his time for a more critical role; secondly, he may have wanted a direct contest with Morarji; and thirdly, he may have wanted to keep himself free for any role that Nehru may have wanted to assign him in the future. Kamaraj was unanimously elected and was seen as a Nehru follower.[68]

Shastri was out of the Cabinet for a very brief while. Within five months of resigning, he was back in the Cabinet under very special circumstances and with a very unique responsibility. The

---

[67]The Syndicate consisted of K. Kamaraj, Atulya Ghosh, Siddavanahalli Nijalingappa, S.K. Patil and N. Sanjiva Reddy.
[68]Brecher, M. (1966). *Succession in India: A Study in Decision-making.* Oxford University Press, p. 19

68th Annual Session of the Congress was held at Bhubaneswar in January 1964. PM Nehru had arrived in the city to attend the AICC session and its preparatory meetings on 6 January. On 7 January, Nehru suffered a stroke and Shastri was asked to share this news with the Subjects Committee, which was then in session. Shastri told the committee of Nehru's indisposition and also relayed the contents of the medical bulletin of the doctors attending on the PM, who stated that he was cheerful and in good spirits. As the Subjects Committee continued its discussions, the responsibility to move the most important resolution at the session—on democracy and socialism—was entrusted to Shastri. Many saw this as a sign of prominence given to Shastri in the Congress hierarchy, even though he was not a Cabinet minister. Shastri also found a place in the new CWC constituted by the party president at the end of the Bhubaneswar session. Shastri's speech, while moving the resolution on democracy and socialism, highlighted that 'Democratic Socialism is the only way through which the country could march towards progress and prosperity, without sacrificing the dignity of the individual.'[69] Defending the public sector, he claimed that it would 'have to grow, as the private sector is incapable of delivering the goods.'

Yet another important development happened during the Bhubaneswar session. Given his failing health, Nehru mentioned to Shastri that he would like to have him back in the Cabinet. This offer was made only to Shastri and not to the other ministers who had resigned under the Kamaraj Plan. When Shastri enquired what his responsibilities would be, Nehru is believed to have told him, 'You will have to do

---

[69]Mankekar, D.R. (1965). *Lal Bahadur: A Political Biography*. Bombay: Popular Prakashan, p. 109

my work'. Shastri's emergence as the clear successor to Nehru became increasingly apparent.[70] The Syndicate is also believed to have played a key role in Shastri's appointment as MWP. Being a group of Congress politicians from outside the Hindi heartland, the Syndicate found Shastri to be more acceptable given his soft nature and stand on the Hindi issue. On the other hand, Morarji was seen as more rigid and took a very strong view in advocating Hindi as the sole official language.

On 22 January 1964, a Rashtrapati Bhavan release announced Shastri's appointment as MWP. It went on to add that he would 'carry out functions entrusted to him by the Prime Minister in relation to the Ministry of External Affairs and the Department of the Cabinet Secretariat and Atomic Energy'. *The Times of India* in its editorial on 24 January 1964 hailed the choice of Shastri and felt that Nehru 'could not have made a better choice'.[71] *The Guardian* in its editorial was more specific on what it felt the new responsibility entailed[72]:

Lal Bahadur Shastri has personal characteristics that might make him the most effective Prime Minister of India. It looks as if Mr Lal Bahadur Shastri is being 'evolved' as the next Prime Minister. The news is welcome for two reasons: first that the problem of succession is at last being tackled and secondly that he is the man in view.

In an article titled 'Political heir to Nehru', H.R. Vohra wrote in *The Guardian* that Shastri was considered by many in the US as a wizard in politics who had the legendary capacity to reconcile differences among people and their opinions.[73]

---

[70] *The Times of India*. (1964, June 2). From microfilms in NML.
[71] From microfilms at NML.
[72] 23 January 1964. From microfilms at NML.
[73] From microfilms at NML.

Shastri had proven his capacities as a negotiator, reconciler and firefighter. Journalist Pran Chopra believed that once he was made MWP, it was clear that he was in line to succeed Nehru as and when the situation arose. His strength lay in the confidence that he would not deviate from the Nehruvian line.

However, his role as MWP remained unclear. He was also ranked fourth in the Cabinet after Gulzarilal Nanda and T.T. Krishnamachari. Even when it came to the Ministries of External Affairs, Cabinet Affairs and Atomic Energy, there were occasions when bureaucrats bypassed Shastri and took the files directly to Nehru. The PM raised no objections to it and Shastri too felt it is was better not to make an issue of it. What Nehru mentioned to him at Bhubaneswar was actually far from practised.

Kuldip Nayar in his memoir, *Beyond the Lines,* refers to two incidents/developments during Shastri's time as MWP. Nayar mentions that Indira Gandhi reviewed all the files that Shastri had made comments on. While Shastri knew of this, he did not protest. He felt that Nehru 'treated him with affection and he did not want to create a situation in which Panditji would have to choose between him and Indira Gandhi'. Possibly, Shastri realized who the choice of PM Nehru would be! On another occasion when Shastri was MWP, Nayar noticed that Shastri had to wait for more than an hour to see Nehru. When Nayar spoke to the private secretary about it, the secretary confided that he has sent the chit up several times but Indira Gandhi has not yet given her consent.

There came a stage, Nayar reports, when Shastri as MWP wished to resign from his position. Nayar says that he told Shastri, 'Nehru has you in mind.' Shastri responded that he 'has his daughter in mind as his successor.' Shastri went on to add that it will not be that easy, and said, 'I am not that much of a sadhu as you imagine, who would not like to be India's Prime Minister.'

A senior civil servant, Dharam Vira, who was close to both Nehru and Shastri, takes an interesting position: 'Nehru had the greatest faith in Shastri and had promoted him in the expectation that he would be a stop-gap Prime Minister who would be favourable to Indira Gandhi when the time comes.'[74] Thus, Shastri's appointment as MWP did send some very clear signals. Shastri, though uncomfortable with the lack of clarity on his ministerial role, and individuals sidestepping his authority, preferred to bide his time and not displease his leader, PM Nehru. His inexhaustible patience ultimately paid off.

An important case he was specifically asked to handle by PM Nehru when Shastri was MWP was the Hazratbal Shrine incident in December 1963. A sacred hair of Prophet Muhammad, preserved for over 300 years at the shrine at Srinagar, J&K, disappeared on 26 December. This caused consternation among not just Muslims but also among the Hindus and Sikhs in Srinagar. There was every chance that the situation could explode into a communal flare-up. The CBI was asked to investigate the disappearance of the sacred relic. In early January of 1964, the relic was mysteriously found in the shrine. The Union home secretary, after discussions with the local authorities, maintained that the culprits who had stolen the relic had 'surreptitiously' placed it back in the shrine as the CBI was close to catching them.

While most people accepted the genuineness of the relic that was recovered, a local action committee (LAC) demanded a special viewing to decide the authenticity of what had been recovered. The state government saw this move as a strategy

---

[74]Srivastava, C.P. (1995). *Lal Bahadur Shastri: A Life of Truth in Politics*, Delhi: Oxford. p. 82

to confront the government and opposed it. In this situation of heightened tensions, Nehru asked Shastri to deal with the situation. The state government and the Union home secretary were not in favour of acceding to the demand of the LAC as they felt it was keen on politicizing the issue and could well complicate the problem. Shastri spoke to the LAC members and found that its leaders were acting with a sense of responsibility. He took the stand that devout Muslims would not question the validity of the relic. He was also convinced of the genuineness of the relic. However, when the LAC leaders assured Shastri that there was no 'politics' in their demand, he announced a special viewing of the relic involving the representatives of the LAC and a panel of moulvis. After some tense moments, those who viewed the relic confirmed that it was genuine, resulting in the crisis being amicably resolved. Shastri won all-round appreciation for having resolved the problem peacefully and to everyone's satisfaction.

J&K also faced a political crisis with the Premier of the state, Khwaja Shamsuddin (a protégé of B.G. Mohammed) becoming very unpopular and not having real control over the administration. Shastri felt that a change of leadership was required to improve the situation in the state. He was also of the view that the change should not be engineered from Delhi but should be initiated from within the state. After holding prolonged discussion with the premier and other senior leaders, he convinced the premier to resign and propose the name of Ghulam Mohammed Sadiq to head the government. Commenting on the smooth transition, Mankekar writes that 'this little man from New Delhi has done the trick with the ease of a David felling a Goliath.'[75] His next move on J&K

---

[75]Mankekar, D.R. (1965). *Lal Bahadur: A Political Biography*. Bombay:

PM Jawaharlal Nehru celebrates Holi at his residence in New Delhi in February 1964. Photo shows (from left to right) Lal Bahadur Shastri, Indira Gandhi and Nehru.

PM Lal Bahadur Shastri delivers his speech at the Non-Aligned Conference in Cairo in October 1964.

The PM broadcasting to the nation in October 1964.

PM Shastri at Palam Airport before taking off for a trip to Maharashtra and Gujarat in October 1964.

PM Shastri garlands the President of India, S. Radhakrishnan.

PM Shastri is seen with Maniben Patel at Navjivan Karyalaya during his visit to Ahmedabad in October 1964.

PM Shastri discusses problems of the world with PM Harold Wilson at 10 Downing Street, London, in December 1964.

PM Shastri being introduced by skipper Raj Singh (in white behind the him) at a Ranji Trophy match between Rajasthan and UP at Allahabad in December 1964.

PM Shastri with the CM of UP, Smt. Sucheta Kriplani, during a visit to the Pali Botanical Research Institute, Lucknow, in December 1964.

The PM on board a plane on his way to Allahabad from Delhi in April 1965.

PM Shastri with Alexei Kosygin, Premier of the USSR, during the former's visit to the USSR in May 1965.

PM Shastri inspects the guard of honour at Kiev Airport during his visit to the USSR in May 1965.

PM Shastri and Field Marshal Ayub Khan of Pakistan talking to each other at 10 Downing Street in London in June 1965.

PM Shastri and President Marshal Tito of Yugoslavia with their wives riding in an electric cart while sightseeing in the island of Vanga in Brijuni, Croatia, in July 1965.

PM Shastri with the Dalai Lama when the latter called on him in New Delhi in October 1965.

Mrs Lalita Shastri (R) mourning her deceased husband, Lal Bahadur Shastri, before his funeral in January 1966.

was to convince PM Nehru to agree to the release of Sheikh Abdullah from imprisonment. His release was a gamble, as one was not sure of the political stand he would take afterwards. He expressed the view that he would like to bring India and Pakistan together on the Kashmir issue and set to work in that direction.

Discussing the Kamaraj Plan and Shastri's return to the Cabinet on Nehru falling ill, Mankekar feels that the 'Kamaraj Plan had ousted the Right, placed the Centre in complete control of the Cabinet and had guaranteed the gaddi [throne] for Mr Shastri.' Commenting on his return as MWP, Mankekar believes that Nehru had made clear his 'chosen heir and successor... [and was] being groomed for Prime Ministership.'[76]

With the PM's health declining, there was a demand for the appointment of a deputy PM. When Nehru had broached the issue with Gulzarilal Nanda, the HM and Number 2 in the Cabinet, he did not receive a favourable response and, so, shelved the idea. Speaking in the Lok Sabha, Nehru said the question of making such an appointment 'has not risen before' him. He went on to add that many of his duties are being 'discharged very efficiently' by his MWP; he was grateful to him and they were 'working very well together'. There could not have been a more direct reference to a successor. Well-known commentator Prem Bhatia felt that the 'succession issue is more or less settled.'[77] He went on to add that Shastri, in keeping with his style, 'does not assert it.' Shastri succeeding Nehru was, for Bhatia, fait accompli.

A few weeks before Nehru's passing away, a public opinion

Popular Prakashan, p. 33

[76]Mankekar, D.R. (1965). *Lal Bahadur: A Political Biography*. Bombay: Popular Prakashan, pp. 23–7

[77]*The Indian Express*. (1964, January 31). From microfilms at NML.

survey was published among a representative sample, to answer the question 'After Nehru, who?'[78] Two questions asked in the study were relevant. Close to three-fourth of the respondents had heard of the recent illness of the PM. When asked from a set of names as to who among them should fill the role of the deputy PM and future PM, Shastri scored over his nearest rival by close to 20 percentage points. If 26.9 per cent favoured Shastri, the next highest support was for Kamaraj at 7.8 per cent. Indira Gandhi came third with 5.9 per cent support and Morarji was much lower at 3.5 per cent. It was becoming increasingly clear that the succession question was more or less settled.

Yet, Shastri was himself more circumspect on the issue. When C.P. Srivastava asked for Shastri's response to the whispers in the corridors of power that he would be the next PM of India, he thought for a moment and admitted that many said that, but the future was unclear and uncertain.

Frank Moraes, writing in 1960, had averred that 'Shastri is very close to Nehru, but he lacks an assertive personality, being of diminutive stature and a retiring disposition.' Moraes went on to add that there could not be 'two men more strikingly different in personality, temperament, training and background,' yet they 'shared the same political outlook, the same social and economic ideals and objectives.' Shastri, he felt, was the quintessential 'home-spun Indian,' unlike Nehru who was an 'amalgam of the ancient and the modern with something simultaneously Eastern and Western.' Did the contrast in their styles and approaches create any friction during the leadership transition when Nehru passed away? How did Shastri carry forward the legacy he inherited even

---

[78] *The Statesman*. (1964, September 10). From microfilms at NML.

as he attempted to carve a niche for himself? This is the focus of the next chapter, which discusses Shastri ascending to prime ministership and leading the country.

4

LEADING A NATION

Ever since he moved to Delhi in 1951, Shastri had slowly but steadily climbed the ladder of power and assumed greater responsibilities with each passing year. From GS of the party to a Cabinet minister responsible for critical portfolios, his was a sharp though steady rise. Even on the two occasions when he resigned from the ministry, he was entrusted with what appeared to be 'tailor-made' party responsibilities that enhanced his role and importance in the party. He was brought back to the Cabinet when his task in the party was successfully completed or when his presence in the government was urgently required. His stint as MWP after PM Nehru fell ill, was, in retrospect, a very carefully designed move to place him in a crucial position when the moment of succession arose.

PM Nehru brought Shastri back to the Cabinet as MWP with the clear instruction that Shastri was expected to do 'all my [Nehru's] work.' While this actually did not happen, Shastri bided his time as was his wont. On 27 May 1964, within four months of Shastri joining back as MWP, PM Nehru passed away. Shastri was present at Nehru's bedside along with Indira Gandhi, Gulzarilal Nanda and T.T. Krishnamachari when the end came. It was indeed the end of an era in Indian politics. The question 'After Nehru, who?' was now not a query for the future but the reality of the present. As Nanda was the seniormost minister in the Nehru Cabinet, he was sworn in as interim PM to carry on the day-to-day responsibilities of the administration and until such time as the CPP chose a new leader. Michael Brecher believes that a 'triumvir' had emerged in the Nehru Cabinet (Nanda, Krishnamachari and Shastri—the three seniormost ministers), which took crucial decisions soon after Nehru passed away. Yet, Brecher maintains that during Nehru's cremation ceremonies, Shastri maintained a 'dignified aloofness'. On the other hand, Brecher believes that Morarji tried to assert his presence, even though he held no formal position in the government, and this was not to the liking of many of those around.[79]

Congress President K. Kamaraj was away in Madras when news of Nehru's health taking a turn for the worse was conveyed to him. He immediately boarded a flight to Delhi, but by the time he landed, the PM had already breathed his last. Kamaraj was taken aback when he heard that Nanda had been sworn in as PM, but was assured that it was an interim arrangement until such time as the CPP chose a new leader. Kamaraj's apprehension was born out of the experience that in politics what was considered temporary often developed the salience of becoming permanent.

THE MOMENT OF TRANSITION

Choosing a successor to Nehru had always been an issue of spirited debate—more outside India than within the country. Now that the country was faced with the 'moment of transition,' the process that was to be followed was closely

[79]Brecher, M. (1966). *Succession in India: A Study in Decision-making.* Oxford University Press, pp. 24, 35–6

watched. Could the polity and the ruling party hold together while taking this momentous decision? This was also a test of the strength of India's democratic character. It has often been contended that moments of transition are the true test of the foundational strength of the democratic process. How India would handle this leadership transition thus, was the spotlight of the world's attention.

Brecher felt that the first PM of India did not consciously name his successor, as he wanted the democratic processes within the party to take that decision. He did provide broad indicators of the possible choices but felt that those leaders need to demonstrate their leadership capacities and emerge on the basis of popular choice.[80] Eminent journalist B.G. Verghese believes that by bringing Shastri back to the Cabinet, Nehru had made a clear indication of his preference of successor, especially keeping in mind Shastri's ideals, integrity and loyalty.

As the country mourned the death of its PM, within the Congress party, informal parleys had begun on the successor to Nehru. The crucial six days—from the day Nehru passed away to the formal announcement of Shastri as the leader of the CPP—saw hectic political activity. Kamaraj played an important role in the process, as V. Balasubramanian reports, with 'amazing fairness and finesse.'[81] A small syndicate had formed around him and they all came to play a critical role in the process. Shastri, in keeping with his style, decided not to take the initiative, did not canvas his candidature and watched from the background. On the other hand, Morarji

---

[80]Brecher, M. (1966). *Succession in India: A Study in Decision-making.* Oxford University Press, pp. 27–8

[81]Balasubramanian, V. "The Best Prime Minister We Have." *Champion of Peace: Tribute to Shastri* by Sudarshan K. Savara, New Delhi: Gyan Mandir 1967, p. 37

and especially his supporters were more vocal in canvassing his candidature for prime ministership.

Those close to Shastri provide an indication of what his thoughts were on the issue. Reference has already been made in earlier chapters to his belief that even as Nehru was alive, he was keen to have Indira Gandhi succeed him. Shastri also felt that this succession (Gandhi's) was fraught with challenges. As mentioned before, in another conversation with aides when he was MWP, he had mentioned that he was 'not a sadhu' to not aspire to be the PM!

When the discussions on the choice of successor began, Shastri is believed to have suggested two names: Jayaprakash Narayan and Indira Gandhi.[82] Both the names were summarily dismissed by Morarji. Shastri himself was especially serious about the second name—Gandhi's. He had made it clear to those close to him, that if Gandhi was keen to lead the nation, he would step back. He confided to Kuldip Nayar that 'if there is a contest, then I can defeat Morarji Desai but not Indira Gandhi.'[83]

Shastri is believed to have met Indira Gandhi and suggested to her, 'Ab aap mulk ko sambhaal leejiye' (Now you please look after the nation). Gandhi is believed to have declined saying that she was still grieving the death of her father and could not even think of taking on the responsibility at that stage. Shastri needed this clarity from her and formally sought it. He was now clear that if Gandhi was not in the race, he would well offer himself as a candidate if the situation so arose.

Morarji's supporters had openly started canvassing for him

---

[82]Srivastava, C.P. (1995). *Lal Bahadur Shastri: A Life of Truth in Politics*, Delhi: Oxford. p. 85

[83]Nayar, K. (2012). *Beyond the Lines: An Autobiography*. Roli Books Private Limited, pp. 178–9

as PM. On the other hand, Shastri remained non-committal. Kamaraj and his syndicate had also become active. Nayar reports that on running into Morarji's son Kanti, he was told, 'Tell your Shastri not to contest.'[84] Around this time, Nayar issued a United News of India press release, which stated that Morarji had thrown his hat into the ring, was clearly a candidate for the post of PM and would not easily withdraw his candidature. The release went on to add that Shastri too was considered another candidate but was reticent and keen to avoid a contest. As this press release went around, it created a mood against Morarji and as a natural corollary, a pro-Shastri sentiment. Nayar reports that when the consensus firmly emerged around Shastri's name, Shastri called him and said, 'No more stories; the contest for leadership is over.' After Shastri's formal selection as the leader of the CPP, Nayar says that Kamaraj acknowledged Nayar's role in the selection and thanked him.

Kamaraj, as Congress president, was keen to avoid a contest for the leadership and wanted a consensus candidate to emerge. This, he said, was vital for a smooth succession. He felt that the task needed to be completed with 'unity and dignity'. A contest would bring with it its attendant acrimony, ill will and bad blood. With the active support of the syndicate, he began discussions within the party on a consensus candidate. The different factions in the party were viewing multiple options in this regard. The leftists and the rightists had their own choices and preferences.

As time progressed, there were only two names being mentioned—Shastri and Morarji. Kamaraj had extensive

---

[84]Nayar, K. (2012). *Beyond the Lines: An Autobiography*. Roli Books Private Limited, pp. 169–70

discussions among Congress leaders. Morarji was known to be a leader with strong likes and dislikes, inflexible in his approach and rigid in his stance. He had a long record of public service and achievement. Successful as the CM of Bombay state (now Mumbai), he had also been an efficient minister for industry and commerce, and later finance. Yet, when he held political office, both in the state and at the national level, he had earned a reputation of being obstinate, uncompromising and unyielding. While his efficiency had earned him many admirers, his apparent 'negative' qualities had also created a formidable set of enemies.

On the other hand, Shastri had no apparent enemies, was seen as a skilled negotiator, a man of principles and someone who reconciled differences. He was also seen as a devout follower of Nehru and his understudy. Moreover, during his tenure as Union HM, he had developed an excellent rapport with the CMs of all the states. After resigning under the Kamaraj Plan, the party work he was entrusted got him in touch with the state units of the Congress party. It was now time to build on the equations he had established and encash on the goodwill he had earned both within the state units of the Congress party and the CMs of the states. This networking—a strength of Shastri's—was something that Morarji had not assiduously cultivated.

Kamaraj and the Syndicate also found it easier to deal with Shastri and were often uneasy with Morarji. Some would even make the point that Kamaraj and the Syndicate felt that Shastri would be more amenable to their ideas and influence. After extensive discussions with party leaders, Congress MPs and the CMs of the states, Kamaraj believed that there was a consensus around the name of Shastri. He conveyed the same to both Morarji and Shastri, and got their consent.

Commenting on Kamaraj's role in the selection of Shastri as the unanimous consensus candidate in a well-managed changeover, Mankekar says that his 'political wisdom, astute statesmanship and masterly handling of a difficult situation... [is what ensured] a smooth, orderly and dignified transition.'[85] Journalist Balasubramanian, who covered the politics beat in those days, believes that Morarji was well aware of the power that the Syndicate had come to wield in the party and was convinced that it would back Shastri if it came down to a contest.[86]

Morarji possibly realized the mood within the party and felt that it was not the appropriate juncture to force a contest. In later years, Morarji would reminisce that Nehru had groomed Shastri to succeed him and had consciously ensured that Morarji was sidelined. The Kamaraj Plan too, he felt in retrospect, was a plan to move him out of the Number 2 position he had come to occupy in the government. When asked to react to Shastri's emerging as a consensus candidate, Morarji said, '[Unless] you feel happy in difficult circumstances, you will never be happy. This is my philosophy in life.'[87] Morarji needed to wait thirteen long years to fulfil his ambition of becoming the PM.

---

[85]Mankekar, D.R. (1965). *Lal Bahadur: A Political Biography*. Bombay: Popular Prakashan, p. 40

[86]Balasubramanian, V. "The Best Prime Minister We Have." *Champion of Peace: Tribute to Shastri* by Sudarshan K. Savara, New Delhi: Gyan Mandir 1967, p. 37.

[87]*The Times of India*. (1964, June 12). From microfilms at NML.

UNANIMOUS ELECTION AS CONGRESS PARLIAMENTARY PARTY LEADER

Shastri was unanimously elected as the leader of the CPP on 2 June 1964, less than a week after the passing away of his mentor, Jawaharlal Nehru. His name was proposed by Gulzarilal Nanda and seconded by Morarji. A week later, on 9 June 1964, Shastri and his Council of Ministers were administered the oath of office. Speaking at the election of Shastri as the new leader of the CPP, Kamaraj, stressing on the changes that a post-Nehruvian Congress would need to adjust to, reminded the party that 'hereinafter it would be impossible for any single individual to discharge the onerous responsibilities that the late Prime Minister had shouldered. It is by collective responsibility, collective leadership and collective approach that you will be able to undertake this task.'

Analysing the Congress strategy in arriving at a consensus on Shastri, Michael Brecher avers that the Congress party was able to ensure a smooth transition without ruffling too many feathers or adversely impacting the unity in the party, while also respecting the popular sentiment in the party.

It is important at this stage to focus on why the Congress and its leadership placed a premium on choosing the successor to Nehru using the consensus framework and avoiding a formal election. It must be underscored that the 'consensus model' has been the preferred instrument of decision-making within the Congress. Most positions that Shastri had occupied within the party were not based on a formal election, but a consensus among the key leaders. Whenever the Congress party had faced an election, it had always been a precursor of strong divisions and splits in the party. The consensus model involved creating a win-win situation. One took all segments of the organization along. It unified the party rather than driving a wedge between groups and factions. It focused on celebrating what was common rather than highlighting what was different.

Yet, the consensus model was also a subtle way of ensuring that the dominant forces within the party manoeuvred its way to ensuring its continued control. Shastri's emergence as a consensus candidate did involve a process of consultation. Critics would also say that it was in order to ensure that the dominant group within the Congress has its way.

In recent times, the consensus model has been reduced to a sham and has undercut genuine internal democracy. Within the Congress party today (and their lead has been followed by other parties too), most decisions are taken by consensus. This includes the choice of CMs. The central leadership is often entrusted with the responsibility of evolving a consensus on who should lead the party and government in a state after an informal consultation with the party's legislators in that state.

There was an interesting episode in a state where the Congress legislature party had to elect its leader. It was decided in the meeting to unanimously pass a resolution requesting the central leadership to name the consensus candidate. The leadership was unable to decide between three key names. As the time of the meeting approached, the observer of the central leadership was given three sealed envelopes that contained the three names with a number on each. The observer was told to contact the high command just before the meeting to ascertain which envelope should be opened to make the announcement. The story doing the rounds is that the observer opened the wrong envelope and the new CM, selected on account of the opening of a faulty envelope, remained in power for a few years!

Soon after his election as the CPP leader, Shastri made a short acceptance speech. He began by saying, 'I tremble when I am reminded of the fact that I have to be in charge of this country and Parliament, which has been led by no less a persona than Jawaharlal Nehru.' He then outlined his priorities. He reminded the Congress MPs that 'our policies have been enunciated and defined and what is essential is their quick and proper implementation.' His commitment to socialism was clear and he went on to add in his acceptance speech that 'in the new social order he had in mind, the few should not be allowed to monopolize the national wealth, leaving others to suffer.'[88]

THE WORLD REACTS

As PM-designate, when Shastri held his first press conference, he outlined three goals that he would prioritize. Firstly, he said that his government would focus on fighting poverty and unemployment. Later, in one of his meetings with the Planning Commission officials, he wanted a new column to be added in all the reports on expenditures, which would include details of the jobs that the said expenditure would create. He went on to highlight the second goal as making national integration an 'irreversible fact'. Finally, he also said his government would concentrate on building the nation's defence strength.

When Shastri's mother heard of his being elected the leader of the CPP and the PM of India, she wished him well and said, '*Main Lal Bahadur se chahti hoon ke jaan chale jaye to jaye, magar desh bana rahe*' (I expect Lal Bahadur to ensure that the country prospers even if he has to sacrifice his life for

---

[88] *The Times of India*. (1964, June 2). From microfilms at NML.

it). She further counselled him 'not to do anything that would cause grief to the poor.'[89]

Michael Brecher outlines five assets that Shastri possessed, which made him the best suitor to be Nehru's successor:

- He hailed from the Hindi heartland, especially UP, which was an asset in terms of the numerical strength of that region in the Lok Sabha.
- His reputation of being unbiased was his prized asset in the leadership race.
- His vast administrative and organizational experience across different levels gave him the much-needed profile to lead the country after Nehru.
- The fact that he was open-minded and a 'centrist' in his ideological approach was also an important plus point.
- His ability and his humility, which allowed ambition to be couched in gentleness, was a vital positive virtue. All these factors placed him at a crucial advantage when the party was looking for a consensus candidate to succeed Nehru.

The New York Times, in a very unique comparison of Shastri and Nehru, reflected that while the former was down-to-earth and grounded in reality, the latter was more often in the philosophical plane without actually coming to seriously interrogate the theoretical economic crises facing the country. If Nehru had his gaze abroad, Shastri was more focused on developments in the country. *The New York Times* also said that, at that time, Shastri's 'hands-on' approach was better suited and more critical to deal with the problems facing the country.[90]

---

[89]Natesan, M. "Prime Minister Lal Bahadur Shastri." *A Study of Lal Bahadur Shastri*, B.S. Gujarati, Delhi: Sterling, 1965, p. 52
[90]From microfilms at NML.

Commenting on Shastri's election, *The Times of India*, in its editorial on 13 June 1964, highlighted that in 'electing Mr Shastri with one voice, the party members have confounded all the gloomy prophets who thought it would have difficulty in answering the fateful question, 'After Nehru, who?'[91] It highlighted that Shastri was always the 'peacemaker' in the Congress party and 'brought the healing touch to bear in resolving several difficult problems in the Congress organization and outside.' Commenting on his first address to the country on becoming the PM, the publication said that 'there was a quality of sincerity and earnestness about Mr Shastri's first broadcast to the nation as PM.' His remark—that 'our way is straight and clear'—won universal appreciation.

Welles Hangen summarized the qualities that had placed Shastri in the leadership position and also provided crucial insights on what to expect in the days ahead[92]:

> Shastri has a will of his own, and what is more unusual, a conscience. Neither is transient... like so many other compromise candidates throughout history, he might well surprise those who chose him, for his apparent pliancy. The mouse might well roar.

On 14 June 1964, *The Times* hailed Shastri's selection as the country placing faith in a 'conciliator', who was a 'craftsman of compromise' and whose 'virtues were political.' Like Harry Truman followed Franklin Roosevelt and Clement Attlee followed Winston Churchill, Shastri seemed to have followed Nehru!

---

[91]13 June 1964. From microfilms at NML.
[92]Hangen, W. "After Nehru, Who?" *Champion of Peace: Tribute to Shastri* by Sudarshan K. Savara, New Delhi: Gyan Mandir 1967, p. 38

CABINET FORMATION: SUBTLE BREAK FROM THE PAST

Having been selected unanimously as the leader of the CPP, Shastri went about the task of constituting his Council of Ministers. He invited Indira Gandhi to join the Cabinet and choose a portfolio of her choice. Many thought she would opt for external affairs and carry on in the footsteps of her father. After a long consultation with her loyalists and supporters, she decided not to opt for this portfolio. She realized that she would be assessed in the context of her father and wanted to avoid any such comparison. Secondly, this portfolio would place her under intense parliamentary scrutiny, something she wished to avoid. She finally opted for information and broadcasting, as it was a sufficiently light portfolio, which would allow her to focus attention on settling several legal and inheritance matters relating to her father, even as she continued to gain visibility on account of the ministry. Shastri readily agreed to the portfolio she sought.

Shastri also invited Morarji to join his Cabinet. While Morarji was willing, there was a hitch. The challenge was not about the portfolio, but related to seniority. Morarji was keen on being Number 2 in the Cabinet after Shastri. On the other hand, Shastri was of the view that as Gulzarilal Nanda had already served as interim PM and had enjoyed the Number 2 status under Nehru, the second slot would need to go to him. Morarji countered that he had been Number 2 in Nehru's Cabinet much earlier than Nanda. Shastri still offered the third slot to Morarji. However, Morarji refused to accept the third position, as he felt it was 'not consistent with my self-respect and dignity.' He thus did not join the Cabinet. Some would believe that if Shastri was keen to accommodate Morarji in the Cabinet, he could well have found a solution, given his special skills at problem-solving. He passed the ball in Morarji's court by offering him a place in the Cabinet but leaving him the choice to refuse to join, unhappy with the rank assigned. By placing the onus on Morarji, Shastri was deftly shielding himself from criticism. Knowing Morarji's inflexibility, rigidity, bluntness and tendency to be unpleasant, Shastri may well have been comfortable with not having to deal with a Cabinet colleague who had the potential to be difficult to deal with. L.P. Singh made a tongue-in-cheek comment on Morarji being kept out, when he said, 'One is reminded of Kant's reference to the crooked timber of humanity out of which no straight thing can be made'.[93]

In the end, the Shastri Council of Ministers was more or less a replica of the Nehru ministry, with three significant additions in the Cabinet—Indira Gandhi, S.K. Patil and N. Sanjiva Reddy. While Gandhi's entry into the Cabinet has already been discussed, Patil and Reddy were important members of the Syndicate within the Congress and their entry indicated the role that this cabal, which included the Congress president, had come to play in the decision-making process in the party.

Commenting on the Shastri ministry, Brecher believes that 'the Shastri Cabinet, like its predecessors, represents the main strands of Indian society and Congress politics.'[94] It provided for a representation of the 'traditionalist-modernist spectrum, regional balance as well as religious inclusion.' This ministry also saw an element of stability during Shastri's tenure as PM for two reasons. Firstly, in the initial phase, Shastri was keen

---

[93]Singh, L.P. (1996). *Portrait of Lal Bahadur Shastri: A Quintessential Gandhian*. Ravi Dayal Publisher, p. 103.
[94]Brecher, M. (1966). *Succession in India: A Study in Decision-making*. Oxford University Press, p. 103

to ensure stability and continuity. Secondly, as time passed, a range of crises (food crisis, language crisis and the India–Pakistan conflict) prevented any tinkering with either the personnel in the ministry or their portfolios.

While Shastri played it safe with the choice of Cabinet ministers, he did assert his role when it came to key portfolios. Given the food crisis gripping the country, Shastri was keen that the portfolio of food be handled by a minister he had full confidence in. He decided to first speak to C. Subramaniam, who was the minister for steel and mines in the Nehru ministry. He decided to call on Subramaniam at his residence. Subramaniam's recollection of the visit highlights the new PM's approach[95]:

> ...immediately after assuming office, [Shastri] visited me at my residence in Delhi—a rare gesture by a Prime Minister... [He requested] that I should be a member of his Cabinet. We discussed the portfolio, and I told him that I would like to continue with my present assignment, because I was in the midst of reorganizing the steel plants and other heavy industries... [He] said he would consider my request.

C.P. Srivastava records that Shastri decided to consider Subramaniam's request and when he could not find another person to head the Food Ministry, he decided to speak to Subramaniam to request him to take charge of the food portfolio. Subramaniam reported on this conversation with Shastri and enquired why his portfolio was being changed. Shastri replied in his disarming simplicity that this portfolio

---

[95]Srivastava, C.P. (1995). *Lal Bahadur Shastri: A Life of Truth in Politics*, Delhi: Oxford. p. 103

has been the nemesis of several stalwarts and he thought Subramaniam was the best suited for it. Subramaniam saw no way to refuse the request.

This was typical of Shastri's style. He left the choice of ministry to Indira Gandhi and got her to decide that she would look after the information and broadcasting portfolio. He offered Morarji a place in the Cabinet, but made it clear that it would be Rank Number 3, leaving it to Morarji to refuse. Later, as Krishnamachari was embroiled in a challenge, he left it to the minister to resign. His way of getting his colleagues to agree with him was by asking them, '*Aap hamaare saath chalenge?*' placing the onus on the one to whom the request was made.

An interesting comparison can be made between G.B. Pant and Shastri. Pant was the CM under whom Shastri started his career in the government as a parliamentary secretary. Pant, it is believed, maintained two diaries. One diary was the formal one, which was to be taken seriously. The second diary was only for making entries in the presence of people and then to be ignored! This was his way of not saying no to anyone. Shastri had a different approach. He used to painstakingly note down, on slips of paper, the requests made by people who came to meet him. He used to stuff these pieces of paper into his pocket and indicate that action would be taken. At the end of the day, he would retrieve these pieces of paper and go through them one by one. The ones that merited action would then be passed on to his assistants, and the rest would be discarded! This was Shastri's way of dealing with requests that came to him.

A major decision that Shastri was required to make was on the appointment of a foreign minister. Nehru had been his own foreign minister and Shastri had to consider whether he himself would like to shoulder the responsibility or assign the portfolio to another minister. After some reflection, Shastri decided to keep the portfolio for himself. Soon after the ministry's formation, Shastri suffered a mild heart attack—the second in less than a decade. Shastri quickly recovered and was back at work very soon. His doctors advised him to forgo the Foreign Ministry and appoint a full-time foreign minister.

Kuldip Nayar recalls a conversation with Shastri in this regard. When asked by Shastri who he could make foreign minister, Nayar first suggested Indira Gandhi's name. Shastri is believed to have replied, 'Nayar sahib, you do not understand politics. She wants to be the prime minister. The portfolio of foreign affairs would make her more important.' Nayar then suggested Mohomedali Currim Chagla's name. However, in the context of India–Pakistan tensions, Shastri did not favour a Muslim at that juncture.[96]

It was after much thought that Shastri decided to recommend to the president the allocation of the external affairs portfolio to Swaran Singh (who was the industry minister) in July 1964. This was a decision taken by Shastri after considering different factors. As the party president, Kamaraj came to know of the new foreign minister a few hours after it was formally announced by the president's office.

In an interview with Mankekar, Shastri highlighted his approach to choosing his Cabinet colleagues[97]:

...the impression has gone around...that I was under the influence of some of the Congress leaders. I can say

[96]Nayar, K. (2012). *Beyond the Lines: An Autobiography*. Roli Books Private Limited, pp. 171–2

[97]Mankekar, D.R. (1965). *Lal Bahadur: A Political Biography*. Bombay: Popular Prakashan, pp. 119–20

without any fear of contradiction, or without any respect to any of my colleagues, that I have not consulted a single person in as far as the formation of my cabinet was concerned. Even additions and alterations were made on my own... In the manner of appointment of ministers of my government, I have been secretive. With apologies to my colleagues, I want to keep this to myself in future also, if and when the occasion arises. It is but natural that I shall take the whole responsibility for this on my shoulders.

While Shastri favoured a consensus approach involving wide-ranging consultations, when it came to matters of Cabinet formation, he clearly preferred to take the final decision himself. In the formation of the first Shastri Cabinet, the changes from the past were more subtle. For the autonomy he gave to his Cabinet ministers, he is often described as a 'non-interventionist Prime Minister.' He did not have a 'kitchen cabinet.' Nayar believes that this style began and ended with him! He gave freedom to his Cabinet ministers to manage their ministries and rarely interfered in their work. Cabinet meetings are also believed to have had more participation and open discussions.

There is another interesting conversation that Nayar refers to in his memoirs.[98] This discussion was with Shastri soon after he had had a heart attack. While praying for Shastri's long life, Nayar mentioned to Shastri that just as there was the question during Nehru's time, 'After Nehru, who?', how would Shastri respond to 'After Shastri, who?' Shastri is said to have thought for a moment and then said, 'If I was to die within one or two years, your Prime Minister would be Indira Gandhi, but

[98]Nayar, K. (2012). *Beyond the Lines: An Autobiography*. Roli Books Private Limited, pp. 171

if I live three or four years...[Yashwantrao Balwantrao] Chavan will be the prime minister.' Shastri's judgement was bang on target. When Nayar mentioned this to Chavan years later, he responded by saying, 'You must write about this in one of your columns.' Chavan went on to become deputy PM for a brief while under Charan Singh's prime ministership (1979–80), but never became the PM.

A DISTINCT APPROACH

Though Shastri had a brief tenure of sixteen months as the PM, during this time he left an indelible stamp of his own distinct approach to leadership and governance. Some of it reflected his personality and style, while the impact of the circumstances under which he assumed prime ministership and the political context of the times were also important factors. During his time as PM, much attention has been focused on his equations with the Congress Party President K. Kamaraj. A question often discussed is: Did Nehru, in the closing years of his prime ministership, have Kamaraj in mind to lead the party and Shastri as the candidate for heading the government? While this did become a reality on Nehru's passing away, it is noticed that in the days of Shastri's prime ministership, the increased role of the Congress president in party affairs was evident. Yet, this did not imply any dilution of the PM's role in managing and running the government. There appeared to be a clear division of powers and responsibilities.

Brecher argues that the pre-eminence of PM Shastri in the power equation was on account of four factors[99]:

[99]Brecher, M. (1966). *Succession in India: A Study in Decision-making.* Oxford University Press, p. 152

- Speaking of Kamaraj, he says, 'Having made a king, the kingmaker lost half his power.'
- Shastri was well aware of the fact that there was genuine support within the party for him to be PM.
- The enormous power and status that the office of the PM involved made Shastri occupy a position of pre-eminence.
- Kamaraj's own style of leadership did not warrant a power struggle with the PM.

A major reform that Shastri introduced as PM was revamping the PM's Secretariat. Lakshmi Kant Jha was brought in as secretary to the PM and given the rank of a secretary of a department. Mindful of the fact that his political stature and experience was much more limited than that of his predecessor, Shastri felt that a strengthened PM's Secretariat was important to ensure a more effective functioning of the government and better coordination between the ministries. Shastri also ensured that there arose no conflict of jurisdiction between the PM's Secretariat and the Cabinet Secretariat. Given the fact that the Cabinet Secretary Dharam Vira and Jha were close friends and had worked together in the past, they ensured that there were no tensions between the two secretariats they headed.

Michael Brecher, in his reflections on the working of the PM's Secretariat, believes that its creation 'marked the accession of influence by the traditional steel frame of [the] Indian government.'[100] Brecher suggests that this was not a new trait demonstrated by Shastri but was visible in his functioning earlier as the HM too. It was, he felt, a 'marked

---

[100]Brecher, M. (1966). *Succession in India: A Study in Decision-making.* Oxford University Press, pp. 115–6

trait of his style, another contrast with his predecessor.' He goes on to add that the PM came under the strong influence of his secretary, Jha.

Based on interviews with Jha, Brecher concludes that the PM's Secretariat emerged as an important power centre under Shastri. Brecher observes that the secretary to the PM, 'rapidly emerged as the most influential civil servant' in the Shastri administration. Shastri's speeches, minutes of meetings, agendas for discussions and points for consideration in decision-making were often prepared by the PM's Secretariat and placed before the PM for his consideration. Jha revealed in his interviews with Brecher that the changes in the PM's Secretariat were on account of both the differences in the decision-making and work style of Shastri and his predecessor, as well as Shastri's not holding multiple portfolios, unlike Nehru. Brecher concludes that 'there is ample evidence to indicate that the Prime Minister's Secretariat...has become a major power centre in all India policies, an interest group in its own right.'

C.P. Srivastava and Kuldip Nayar strongly differ from Brecher's perspective on the subject.[101] They are of the view that Shastri's style of decision-making was more consultative and involved detailed discussions. Given this approach, it may appear that the PM was increasingly dependent on his Secretariat and more critically his secretary. Yet, both Nayar and Srivastava give indications of how Shastri would read drafts put up to him, make significant changes, and at times even send them back to be redrafted. Shastri was of the firm

---

[101]Nayar, K. (2012). *Beyond the Lines: An Autobiography*. Roli Books Private Limited, pp. 175–6

Srivastava, C.P. (1995). *Lal Bahadur Shastri: A Life of Truth in Politics*, Delhi: Oxford. pp. 106–7

belief that the ultimate responsibility for decisions made must rest with him, and his approach to decision-making reflected this conviction. His consultative nature and yen for hearing out all viewpoints could have given the impression that he was influenced by others; yet, it is clear that the final decisions were often taken by him after taking into account all the perspectives and views expressed before him.

Srivastava recalls an important episode when he joined the PM's Secretariat as the joint secretary.[102] When inviting Srivastava to join his team, Shastri mentioned that the 'job of a prime minister is difficult, but not impossible. Let us try. If we succeed, well and good. If I fail, I will resign and go.' The use of 'we' and 'I' was typical of Shastri's style. He used to say, 'we succeed' and 'I fail,' thus making it clear that he would take the onus of failure and share the credit for success with everyone involved.

CRITICAL OF BUREAUCRACY

Shastri's relation with the bureaucracy has been a major focus of debate.[103] Those who believed that he was dependent on the civil servants during the many ministerial positions he occupied, are possibly mistaking his desire for consultation as representing a heavy reliance on officialdom.

L.P. Singh, who watched him from close quarters, recalls that Shastri often sought the views of officials 'more as a sounding board' for his ideas. Singh goes on to add that Shastri never drew officials into a political discussion. Shastri

---

[102]Srivastava, C.P. (1995). *Lal Bahadur Shastri: A Life of Truth in Politics*, Delhi: Oxford, p. 8

[103]Singh, L.P. (1996). *Portrait of Lal Bahadur Shastri: A Quintessential Gandhian*. Ravi Dayal Publisher, p. 27

was often critical of the civil services.[104] In a press conference, he once conceded, 'I know that the administration has yet to gear up to the need of the situation... There is delay in the disposal of papers or disposal of cases, sometimes our procedures cause delay... Recommendation plays an important role.'[105] Zeroing in on officers, he said that they can 'quote things admirably well but the point is whether they can bring about a change in the existing situation... I find that a mediocre like me is able to produce something new and original... [The] officers who are far, far abler than myself go on with their routine way of thinking and perhaps routine way of working.' Thus, while he was critical of the approach of the civil servants, he was aware of the wealth of experience they possessed and gave them due credit.

During his tenure as PM and even earlier as a minister both at the centre and in UP, Shastri paid special attention to the fight against corruption in the administration. While conceding that one can 'certainly reduce corruption but can't eliminate it completely', he did make a sincere attempt to deal with the problem. As mentioned earlier, during his tenure as the Union HM, he was instrumental in the appointment of the Santhanam Committee to suggest measures to tackle corruption and streamline the administration. As PM, he implemented the Santhanam Committee report and the provisions that ensured that government servants were required to carry out only legal orders, whereby the failure to act as per one's own best judgment was considered as misconduct. As PM, he also constituted the Administrative Reforms Commission under the chairmanship of Morarji and

---

[104] *The Times of India*. (1962, April 30). From microfilms at NML.
[105] Ibid.

gave it a mandate to suggest a comprehensive review of the administrative system.

FOOD CRISIS TO GREEN REVOLUTION

Two major challenges that Shastri was required to handle soon after taking over as the PM were the food and language crises. The manner in which Shastri dealt with both these developments reflected his modified style of functioning. It indicated both the democratic nature of Cabinet decision-making as well as an increased role for CMs in national politics. The greater involvement of CMs could well be a corollary to the important role they played in the choice of Shastri as the successor to Nehru.

The manner in which Shastri dealt with the food crisis merits detailed elaboration. The initial years after Independence saw a specific focus on heavy industry development. In the process, the emphasis that should have been given to agriculture was ignored. The cumulative impact of this was seen in the 1960s, with the sharp rise in foodgrain import. To add to his challenges, the year that Shastri took over as PM saw a bad monsoon, which further aggravated the food problem. Food prices had risen by 22 per cent in a period of eighteen months. This increase equalled what had been seen over the previous decade. The hoarding of foodgrains by traders in anticipation of a better price had created a food scarcity and the government had not taken adequate measures to address the problem.

As part of its efforts to deal with the hoarders, the Essential Commodities (Amendment) Act was promulgated. This provided for strict penalties for hoarding foodgrains. Yet, the powers vested by the ordinance were hardly invoked out of fear of antagonizing an important and influential segment of society.

As part of the revised fourth Five-Year Plan, Shastri ensured that the highest priority was accorded to agriculture and increased the base of foodgrain production. Yet, Shastri needed to tread carefully on the matter, as in the distribution of powers between the centre and the states, 'food' was under the state governments. He actively involved the CMs in the major decisions that were taken on the agricultural front. Given the need for the proactive involvement of the state governments in resolving the food imbroglio, the consultation and participation of the CMs in decision-making were vital. *The New York Times* highlighted the strengths of Shastri's approach when it said that the 'principle of political collectivity, which seems to be installing itself in the new Government, is illustrated by the decision to call together the chief ministers of the 16 states to work out nationwide anti-inflation measures in the food market.'[106]

Shastri had handpicked C. Subramaniam as the food minister to deal with this crisis. As PM, Shastri extended full support to him to deal with the grave food situation. The Food Ministry under Subramaniam, with the support of Shastri, initiated a range of measures to help overcome the emergency situation caused by the scarcity of foodgrains. These steps reflected a comprehensive approach to resolving the challenge. The government realized that to expand the availability of foodgrains, their import needed to be focused on. While this met with some opposition from Shastri's Cabinet colleagues (especially Finance Minister T.T. Krishnamachari), Shastri unequivocally supported the measure and got Cabinet approval

---

[106] *The New York Times*. (1964, June 7). From microfilms in the NML.

for the same. With the active support of the governments of the US, Canada and Australia, the import of foodgrains did help tide over the crisis.

Subramaniam, as food minister, initiated a three-pronged strategy to deal with the food crisis. This scheme involved an integrated approach to production, distribution and pricing. Several long-term measures to deal with the situation were also outlined. He involved agricultural experts, who had field experience, to help drive and implement the new policy. He also brought to the Agriculture Ministry, senior All India Services (AIS) officers from the states, who had rich experience in managing agriculture at the ground level. Whenever there were challenges with the state governments in securing the deputation of officers, the PM intervened to convince the CMs to release the said officers.

The ministry also focused attention on strengthening research in the field of agriculture. The pay scales and service conditions of agricultural scientists were greatly improved to attract the best talent pool. The Indian Council for Agricultural Research was also established as a nodal agency to coordinate research in the field of agriculture.

Keeping in mind the need for an effective network to make foodgrains available to people in remote areas and villages, Shastri initiated steps to expand the network of fair price shops across the country. In 1963, it was estimated that the food subsidy, through the fair price shops, was around ₹37 crore. This was expected to rise to ₹50 crore in 1964. Shastri also got the Agricultural Commission constituted. This commission was tasked with constantly monitoring and reviewing the price situation. It was also asked to set reasonable margins for prices at wholesale and retail levels.

Besides these, Shastri established the Food Grains Trading

Corporation. This corporation was assigned the responsibility of purchasing internal produce at remunerative rates and ensuring their proper distribution. This improved procurement price for foodgrains was an inducement to farmers.

The government realized that to make agriculture attractive, it was vital that farmers produce more yield per acre. Shastri got the relevant department to prioritize intensive irrigation. Plant protection measures were also strengthened. Legislation was introduced for quality control of imported seeds to increase agricultural yield. The use of scientific methods in agriculture was also encouraged. An important initiative was the establishment of 1,000 plots of 5 acres each for growing wheat. Modern scientific techniques and methods were employed to demonstrate to farmers the benefits of new technology. This was later replicated in rice-growing areas, and several rice mills were opened across the country. All these measures paved the way for ushering in the Green Revolution.

At an emotional level, Shastri advised citizens to sacrifice one meal a day to help tide over the food crisis. 'If one gives up one meal in a day, some other person gets his only meal of the day,' was his appeal to people. To set an example, his family stopped having one meal a day. While this step was a laudable gesture to be one with the challenge that the country faced, it is unclear as to how giving up a meal would actually help another family. There was no corresponding effort to actually ensure that the one meal that a family did not have was actually passed on to a family that was struggling to have even a single meal. The challenge involved a combination of poverty as well as non-availability of foodgrains, and one is not certain how abstinence from consumption of a meal would automatically help a needy family. It, of course, could be argued that in the context of foodgrain scarcity, avoiding a meal would allow the scarce foodgrains to be consumed by others. Yet, the strategy for the effective distribution of the scarce foodgrains as well as the affordability of the same would have remained a key concern.

Steps to initiate a 'White Revolution' (as it later came to be called) were taken during Shastri's premiership. In October 1964, on a visit to a unit of Anand Milk Union Limited—or Amul, as it is more popularly known—located at Anand, Gujarat, Shastri lauded its success and advised everyone to emulate its achievements. After a long discussion with Chairman Dr Verghese Kurien, who played a key role in the Amul experiment, Shastri accepted his suggestion to establish a National Dairy Development Board (NDDB) to monitor dairies across the country. Dr Kurien accepted Shastri's suggestion that he should head the NDDB and, in return, placed a condition that the Board be headquartered at Anand, which Shastri readily agreed to. The NDDB was formally established in 1965.

TEST OF STRENGTH, CAPACITY AND LEADERSHIP

Soon after coming to power, the Shastri government faced its first NCM in the Lok Sabha. Moving the motion in the Lok Sabha on 11 September 1964, Opposition stalwart Nirmal Chandra Chatterjee stated that he was 'constrained to move this motion because of the mounting misery of the common man in the country and the crisis [that] existed in every sphere—social, political and economic.' The criticisms of the Opposition were many: the food crisis, the increasing corruption, the drift in the administration, the delays in decision-making and the charge of deviation from Nehruvian policies.

Commenting on the introduction of the NCM, *The Statesman*, in its editorial, wrote[107]:

> While allowances must be made for the strong feelings created over the setback in food, prices, policy and planning, none but the most uncharitable can say that the Shastri Cabinet has failed to tackle them in real earnest; proofs of performance so far available are not so inadequate as to warrant an outright condemnation.

Commenting on the issues raised by the Opposition in the NCM, journalist Inder Malhotra reflected that Shastri faced the Parliament with confidence. Malhotra went on to add that many of the Opposition's charges of corruption required a firm response from the PM as the leader of the nation. If there was justification in the charges, then action against the guilty were warranted. If the charges were untrue, those who made the charges should be held accountable. Malhotra made a case for immediate measures to be taken.

Thus, as the debate began in the Lok Sabha, there was praise for the earnest efforts made by the government under Shastri's leadership. Yet, there was also an expression of impatience that the government was not taking the required decisions in right earnest. It was also felt that the PM must provide the direction and lead the way. As the debate proceeded, Hirendranath Mukherjee, the veteran Communist leader, called Shastri a man with a 'split personality' who officially said he followed Nehru but did not do so in practice, and had deviated quite substantially from the Nehruvian line.

PM Shastri responded in strong words to the comments of Mukherjee in his reply to the debate. While deflecting attention

---

[107] *The Statesman*. (1964, September 9). From microfilms in the NML.

away from the former PM, in his typical style, he took the responsibility for his government's actions. He stressed on the need for a new way of thinking and flexibility to chart one's own course. Shastri asserted that he would not like to take refuge in Nehru for covering his own lapses.

Commending the reply that Shastri gave to the NCM, the political correspondent of *The Statesman* felt that the PM's frankness and open approach won the support of the members of the House. The NCM was defeated. The paper also highlighted how the NCM gave Shastri an opportunity to assert his leadership and emerge out of the shadow of Nehru[108]:

> Not a day too soon, Mr Lal Bahadur Shastri staked his claim to be himself. He told the Lok Sabha…in no uncertain terms but with utmost respect for Nehru that he would like his politics to be judged on their own and not by the degree of their conformity with Mr Nehru. A real leader, he said, does not tread the beaten path. He responds to change and demands the right to do so himself.

This first NCM was indeed moved within three months of Shastri becoming the PM. It was indeed a test of his strength, capacity and leadership. The two major accusations against the government, launched by the Opposition, were on Shastri's in capacity to take quick decisions and the departures that he had initiated from the Nehruvian path. Shastri addressed both the issues in his inimitable style. He was not endowed with oratorical skills to hold an audience spellbound like his predecessor, but he compensated for it with the sincerity of

---

[108]19 September 1964. From microfilms at NML.

his words and the earnestness of his intentions. He made a genuine attempt to dispel the image of being a leader unable to take quick and firm decisions. He was swift to point out that his style was different from his predecessor. He spent a greater amount of time in dialogue and consultation, but when the situation warranted, he could take immediate action. He had the honesty and humility to concede his mistakes and strongly defend his actions as PM, without being disrespectful to Nehru. Believing that every leader ought to adopt a style and approach that suited his/her temperament and attitude, he sought to take ownership of his faults and failures, and deftly moved the attention away from his predecessor. As the media highlighted, the PM made a concerted attempt to seek a vote of confidence not on the basis of what he inherited but for what he authentically had come to represent.

TACKLING CRISES HEAD-ON

A major crisis that PM Shastri faced was the anti-Hindi agitation in the Madras state. When the Constitution was adopted on 15 January 1950, the provisions relating to the official language of the Union stated that it shall be Hindi in the Devanagari script. It went on to add that 'for a period of fifteen years from the commencement of this Constitution, the English language shall continue to be used for all the official purposes of the Union.' The constitutional provisions also stated that the 'Parliament may by law provide for the use, after the said period of fifteen years, of the English language.'

When the language agitation broke out in Madras over the apprehension that Hindi would be imposed on the South, Shastri, the then HM, was deputed to Madras by PM Nehru to resolve the issue. Based on his discussions with the agitators, the OLA was piloted in the Parliament by Shastri and approved by the former. It provided that from 25 January 1965, English may continue to be used, in addition to Hindi, for all official purposes of the Union. Nehru held out the assurance in the Parliament that Hindi would never be imposed on any part of the country and English would continue to be used until such time as the non-Hindi speaking states wanted it. The provisions of the OLA, read with the assurances of the PM, had in a sense settled the matter.

As 25 January 1965 approached, two types of developments queered the pitch. First, the belligerence and attitude of the Hindi fanatics, who seemed hell-bent to make Hindi the sole official language of the Union. The Union Public Service Commission, more popular as the UPSC, had given clearance to the AIS examinations to be written in Hindi. While this had not been implemented till then, it had created quite some apprehension, especially in the South. Second, political developments in the state of Madras need to be taken into account. The DMK was emerging as a major political force in opposition to the Congress party, which was the ruling party in the state. The DMK saw the potential of an anti-Hindi agitation in whipping up public sentiments.

This was the environment that the country faced as it approached 25 January. While there were tensions below the surface, it had not presented itself in any visible signs of protest up till then. What triggered off the protest was an elaborate press briefing by officials of the MHA on 24 January 1965. At this press meet, officials spoke of the 'likely enhanced use of Hindi in administrative matters from 26 January, when Hindi would become the official language of the Union.' The fact that this change would be gradual appeared to have been stated as a belated afterthought. The newspapers covered the press meet the next day, focusing on the 'enhanced use of Hindi'. Student protests broke out all over Madras state, inspired by the principal Opposition party, the DMK. Some reports also indicated that the DMK spread word that English was to be replaced by Hindi.

What further heightened the crisis was an instruction issued by the Ministry of Information and Broadcasting that some circulars would be sent out henceforth in Hindi only.[109] Michael Brecher is of the view that this crisis was the byproduct of the mishandling of the communication on the government campaign and the preparation for the changeover.

Demonstration soon broke out across the Madras state, resulting in a fatality, a few self-immolations and the arrest of thousands of protestors. PM Shastri was deeply distressed by the developments and made an appeal to the protestors: 'I cannot understand why people should kill themselves for something which should pose no problem at all. We do not want to impose any language on any part of the country.'[110] The PM reiterated the provisions of the OLA and Nehru's assurance on the floor of the Lok Sabha.

The PM was informed that the agitation had died down after his assurances. Yet, the DMK saw an opportunity to carry forward the agitation for political gains. On 10 February 1965, violent agitations broke out in different parts of the state of Madras. There was police firing in which nineteen people were killed. The violence continued unabated the next day too. Shastri had decided to address the nation on the evening of 11 February. The Food and Agriculture Minister, C. Subramaniam, who hailed from Madras, favoured a

---

[109]This was issued without the consent of the Minister of Information and Broadcasting, Indira Gandhi.

[110]*The Indian Express.* (1965, January 28). From microfilms at NML.

'statutory basis' for implementing the assurances given by PM Nehru in the Parliament. Some ministers felt that this should be done in consultation with the leaders of the Hindi-speaking states. Unhappy with this attitude, Subramaniam submitted his resignation to the PM.

In his address to the nation, Shastri reiterated the provisions of the OLA and the assurances given by Nehru to the Parliament. He felt that the apprehensions that had led to the agitation were based on an unfortunate misunderstanding of the factual position.

He highlighted four points:

- Each state of the Union would have the full freedom to continue its official work in a language of its choice— either the regional language or English.
- Interstate communication could either be in English or, if in Hindi, should be accompanied by a proper translation in English. Further, English translations will be available of Hindi communications addressed to the centre by any state.
- Non-Hindi states have every right to correspond with the centre in English.
- English will continue to be used by the central government in the transactions of business. The PM concluded his address to the nation by expressing his distress about an agitation being launched 'without any attempt to discuss.' He emphasized the need to maintain the unity of the country even as one recognized the multiple diversities present.

The PM's speech did have a sobering effect; yet, there was a new challenge in the form of Subramaniam's resignation. Another minister from Madras state, Ozhalur Viswanatha

Alagesan also submitted his resignation. Next day, the newspapers gave more coverage to the resignations than to the PM's speech. The state-wide agitation in Madras continued, resulting in more fatalities and self-immolations.

The PM finally decided to convene a meeting of all CMs and spoke to each of them individually. It was becoming increasingly evident that a statutory basis for the assurances of Nehru in the Parliament was needed. Shastri was keen to arrive at this conclusion based on a consensus among the CMs. He was also preparing the ground for an alternative measure—amending the OLA. The Cabinet then discussed two alternative proposals: a formal resolution of the Parliament, incorporating Nehru's assurances; and the modification of the OLA. The two ministers, Subramaniam and Alagesan, withdrew their resignations.

After the CMs' conference and the CWC meeting, the consensus emerged that the OLA needed to be amended. At the CMs' conference, there was no opposition to this proposal from the CMs of the Hindi-speaking states. However, at the CWC meeting, Morarji, Jagjivan and Ram Subhag Singh opposed any amendment to the law. The CWC finally endorsed the amendment to the law. The Parliament then approved the amendments to the OLA, putting an end to the crisis.

Shastri's handling of the crisis involved sustained discussions and negotiations on this sensitive emotional issue. Creating the grounds for a consensus involved patience and reconciling what appeared as irreconcilable positions. Shastri's opponents among the senior leaders in the Congress party did try to make the situation difficult for the PM. Morarji not only opposed the move in the CWC, but had made a speech at Ahmedabad saying that 'we should immediately switch over the Hindi in the central administration and the regional languages in the states.'[111] Jagjivan too had expressed himself against the PM's proposal. Shastri did not confront his opponents but allowed a consensus to emerge after sustained discussions. It needs to be stressed that under Shastri's leadership, the CWC became a more genuine platform for deliberation, dialogue and decision-making.

At the other end, the DMK had hoped to make the anti-Hindi issue the plank for its 1967 Assembly election campaign to unseat the Congress government. In spite of the assurances given in 1963, the DMK preferred to exploit the issue to its advantage. They were ably assisted by the Hindi zealots at the central level, who raised all types of apprehensions through their actions and statements. Shastri was required to navigate a solution, dealing with all these contradictions. Dousing the fires caused by the language agitation was one of the PM's major successes.

Michael Brecher is of the view that the PM's approach to decision-making and the 'new equilibrium of power in all-India affairs has led to short-term tranquillity at the probable cost of long-term disunity.'[112] This is an unfair criticism, as it does not take into account the need at that time to balance diverse and often conflicting interests. The long-term consequences could well be on account of the play of politics, and the approach and stand adopted by leaders in the post-Shastri period.

---

[111]Srivastava, C.P. (1995). *Lal Bahadur Shastri: A Life of Truth in Politics*, Delhi: Oxford. pp. 130–1

[112]Brecher, M. (1966). *Succession in India: A Study in Decision-making*. Oxford University Press, p. 167.

5

JAI JAWAN, JAI KISAN:
THE ESSENCE OF INDIA'S SOUL

Shastri's premiership is often divided into two phases. During his first year in office, Shastri dealt with several serious domestic challenges. It looks as if he was moving from crisis to crisis, on constant firefighting mode. By the May of 1965, a serious crisis and confrontation was brewing at the border with Pakistan. This then became his primary concern during the rest of his prime ministership. This phase saw Shastri truly demonstrate his firmness, determination and leadership skills, and changed the way people in India and abroad viewed his stewardship.

During Shastri's premiership, Pakistan indulged in a major military adventure with India. On assuming office as the PM, Shastri, in his first address to the nation, had held out the hand of friendship by saying[113]:

> ...for too long, India and Pakistan have been at odds with each other... [We] must reverse the tide. This will require determination and good sense on the part of the governments and people of both India and Pakistan. President Ayub Khan's recent broadcast has showed both

---

[113] *The Times of India*. (1964, June 12). From microfilms at NML.

wisdom and understanding... However, a great deal of patience will be necessary.

Shastri wished to carry forward the initiatives taken by Nehru to build bridges of peace with Pakistan. Yet, the 1962 experience with China weighed heavily on Shastri's mind and convinced him of the need to act with caution when it came to Pakistan. During the above-mentioned address, he referred to China as well: 'China has wronged us and deeply offended our Government and people by her premeditated aggression against us. Despite our strongest feelings about this aggression, we have shown our desire for a peaceful settlement.'

In October 1964, Shastri made an unscheduled stopover at Karachi on his return from Cairo after attending the Non-Aligned Movement summit. Pakistan's President Ayub Khan is reported to have said to his foreign minister, Zulfikar Ali Bhutto, on his proposed meeting with Shastri, 'This little man—what will I speak to him?' Yet, Shastri's meetings with Pakistani leaders were held in a warm and cordial atmosphere. The statement issued at the end of the visit made three important points:

- The relations between the two countries need to be improved to their mutual advantage.
- The outstanding problems should be resolved in an honourable, peaceful and equitable manner.
- Discussions between the two governments should be resumed at the appropriate level.

The first signs of trouble began with Pakistan's intervention in the Rann of Kutch (RoK) region of Gujarat. The Pakistani forces made a few intrusions into Indian Territory. India came up with a muted response to the Pakistani incursions. This, many believed, emboldened Pakistan, which misread the Indian hesitance. Both Indian intentions and the capacity of its leadership were grossly underestimated by Pakistan.

L.P. Singh suggests that in the eyes of Pakistan, Shastri was 'considered incapable of holding the country together or providing decisive leadership.'[114] Singh refers to the report submitted by the outgoing Indian high commissioner to Pakistan, Gopalaswami Parthasarathy, in which reference is made to a conversation he had with Bhutto during a farewell meeting. Bhutto spoke of the 'impending disintegration of India.' After scanning the report, Shastri is believed to have remarked that it is 'Pakistan and not India, which was heading towards disintegration.' This exchange is indicative of both the attitude of the Pakistani leadership and the response of the Indian PM.

Pakistan's claim was for some of the territories of the RoK, which they claimed were under India. Shastri made it clear in a statement in the Parliament on 3 May 1965: 'The Kutch–Sind border is a well-defined, well-known and well-established border. A larger part of the boundary is not demarcated on the ground. This is so, however, because there is no disputed boundary between the Province of Sind and the Kutch durbar.' Speaking later at Hyderabad, Shastri reiterated the point that India was for exploring a peaceful solution but 'will have to act as the situation demands.'

The PM of the UK, James Harold Wilson, sought to de-escalate the tensions between India and Pakistan and came up with a set of proposals. There was a heated debate in the

---

[114]Singh, L.P. (1996). *Portrait of Lal Bahadur Shastri: A Quintessential Gandhian*. Ravi Dayal Publisher, pp. 26–7

Parliament on the issue, with members demanding details of the Wilson proposals. Shastri responded to the debate by informing the House that the British PM had indeed made a set of proposals, but 'it will not be in public interest to spell out the details.'[115] In a rare reaction, Shastri raised his voice and went on to add:

> I want members of the opposition to remember that we on this side also know something of the national honour and how to protect it. Just four of five people alone cannot claim to be its sole custodians... I want to make it absolutely clear that to run the government is our responsibility and we are going to discharge it. We do take broad guidance from this house on matters of policy. But we cannot be given executive directions every day. It would be an impossible situation and I cannot accept it.

THE TALLEST DECISIONS BY THE SHORTEST MINISTER

Shastri displayed quiet firmness and willingness to take the battle into the Opposition camp if the situation so warranted. He had set into place a consultative mechanism that involved senior members of the Cabinet, prominent party leaders and key members of the Opposition. It was becoming increasingly clear that the Pakistanis have a much bigger game plan that focused on Kashmir. It afterwards became clear that it was a four-phase plan, the first of which involved the actions in the RoK, titled 'Operation Desert Storm'. On 1 July 1965, India and Pakistan agreed to restore the status quo ante as on 1 January, and this brought a temporary end to the cross-border

---

[115]*Hindustan Times*. (1965, May 1). From microfilms at NML.

exchanges. Shastri was clear that India would be focused on peace and he was willing to adopt an approach of flexibility without compromising on India's national interests. In an address to the nation explaining the ceasefire, he told the people that a grave situation was not allowed to go out of control.

It was clear that the ceasefire was a lull before the impending storm. Shastri was constantly briefed by the army commanders of the situation on the ground. Even as the ceasefire had been accepted by Pakistan, they had been planning Phase II, which was titled 'Operation Gibraltar'. The RoK exercise was, for Pakistan, a testing of the waters on India's response to incursions and the response of its leadership. Operation Gibraltar involved sending Pakistani forces as 'raiders' into India and creating ferment in Kashmir by projecting the unrest as actions by the locals for the 'liberation' of Kashmir. The second phase of the approach was launched by Pakistan on 5 August.

Shastri adopted a four-fold strategy to deal with the situation:

- The Cabinet was kept fully informed of all developments. Given that the infiltrations were occurring in J&K, the government there was also taken into confidence.
- During regular discussions with military commanders, the responsibility to defend India's territories and remain in a state of preparedness was underscored.
- It was decided not to approach the United Nations (UN), as it was an internal matter relating to protecting India's territory and interests. This was an important and significant departure from the Nehruvian practice.

• Shastri also decided to brief the country by regularly addressing the nation.

On the day Pakistan launched Operation Gibraltar, Shastri gave clear instructions to the services chiefs, '*Badhe chalo, bahaaduro*' (March on, brave soldiers). In his address to the nation on 12 August, Shastri told his fellow citizens that the Pakistani infiltration was a 'thinly disguised armed attack on the country.' He was also critical of the Pakistani propaganda and the misinformation they were circulating as being 'blatantly and completely untrue.' In one of his strongest censuring of the Pakistani leadership, he said that 'when freedom is threatened and territorial integrity is endangered, there is only one duty—the duty to meet the challenge with all our might.' He reiterated this point in his Independence Day address on 15 August 1965, where he maintained that 'Pakistan will not be allowed to take even an inch of our territory in Kashmir.' This hardening of the PM's position was clearly evident and was a direct response to the actions by Pakistan.

Outlining his approach to the RoK episode and subsequent developments, Shastri told Kuldip Nayar[116]:

> Pakistan misunderstood my desire not to fight as a sign of weakness. It thought that I would never go to war and Pakistan tried to take undue advantage in Kashmir. When it did so, I was convinced that Pakistan was not serious about good relations and peace with India. I decided to act.

The 1962 debacle with China was constantly on the minds of the common people as well as the leadership. Shastri ensured

---

[116]Nayar, K. (2012). *Beyond the Lines: An Autobiography*. Roli Books Private Limited, p. 181

that the forces acted proactively to deal with any situation. The infiltrators were dealt with effectively and neutralized before they could ferment any crisis and trigger off a rebellion. In an interview to *The New York Times* on 22 August 1965, Shastri made it clear that 'if Pakistan continued her aggression, India would not limit herself to defensive measures, but would strike back.' Nayar says that the swiftness with which Shastri responded to the developments with Pakistan took many by surprise and demonstrated the firmness of his resolve and determination to deal with any eventuality.

Around this time, even as tensions with Pakistan were mounting, Shastri's government faced an NCM in the Lok Sabha. This was the second such motion against his government. The focus of the Opposition was twofold—rescind the agreement with Pakistan relating to the RoK and adopt a much tougher stance on Pakistan. At the start of the debate, Shastri had secured the full support of the Congress MPs for his initiatives. He strongly defended the agreement on the RoK and did not, at this stage, want to be seen as violating an international agreement. He reiterated his stand on Pakistan as evidenced in his address to the nation, where he had made clear that force would be met by force. The NCM was defeated. The debate once again demonstrated Shastri's leadership skills, as he defended his actions with firmness in the face of a crisis.

Pakistan launched the third phase of their operation, titled 'Operation Grand Slam' on 1 September 1965. Their game plan had been that if Operation Gibraltar succeeds, they would have caused enough unrest in Kashmir to launch a full-scale attack in the region. In spite of the limited success of Operation Gibraltar, Pakistan went ahead with Operation Grand Slam. Shastri immediately convened a meeting of the army and air force chiefs and, with the defence minister, spelt out clearly India's strategy:

- To defeat Pakistan's attempt to seize Kashmir by force and make it abundantly clear that Pakistan would never be allowed to wrest Kashmir from India.
- To destroy the offensive power of Pakistan's armed forces.
- To occupy only minimal Pakistani territory to achieve these purposes, which would be vacated after the satisfactory conclusion of the war. The third element of the plan, which was a key part of the strategy, was kept under wraps and would be operationalized at the appropriate moment.

India was also coming under tremendous international pressure to de-escalate tensions. Shastri made it clear to foreign heads of state through India's diplomatic missions abroad that, while India wanted peace, it was Pakistan that had provoked the crisis and India would defend its interests. In a response to the UN Secretary-General U Thant, who made an appeal to both India and Pakistan to cease hostilities, Shastri clarified India's position[117]:

There is no other name for the massive Pakistani infiltrations across the Ceasefire Line...that Pakistan has launched into our territory, but aggression. The aggression throws on us, a sovereign State, responsibilities for defence which is our right and duty to discharge... I trust that, in the first instance, you will ascertain from Pakistan if it will accept the responsibility

---

[117]*Indo-Pakistan Conflict*, Security Council Documents, September 1965, Delhi: Government of India, pp. 13–4

for withdrawing not only its armed forces but also the infiltrators and for preventing further infiltrations.

There was hectic international activity to try and end the hostilities in the subcontinent. The UN passed a resolution on 3 September 1965, calling upon both India and Pakistan to take steps for an immediate ceasefire. India made its stand clear that Pakistan withdraw its offensive and take responsibility for the infiltrators. Shastri spelt out India's stand in an address to the nation. He asserted that 'India cannot simply go from one ceasefire to another and wait till Pakistan chooses to start hostilities again... [W]hat we are up against is a regime which does not believe in freedom, democracy and peace as we do.'

INDIA'S FIRST SURGICAL STRIKE

Meanwhile, the Pakistani actions at the border as part of Operation Grand Slam were increasing. On 6 September, India decided to put into action its third part of the plan—to occupy only minimal Pakistani territory to achieve these purposes, which would be vacated after the satisfactory conclusion of the war.

Kuldip Nayar had a detailed discussion with Shastri on this decision, long after the conclusion of the war[118]:

After the war, I asked Shastri ['Who] gave the specific order to cross the international boundary[?'] 'I did', he said. According to Shastri, Chaudhuri[119] and others were taken aback when he asked them to march into Pakistan.

---

[118]Nayar, K. (2012). *Beyond the Lines: An Autobiography*. Roli Books Private Limited, p. 185

[119]The then chief of the army staff, Jayanto Nath Chaudhuri.

Harbaksh Singh[120] told me that the army would never forget 'this tallest decision by the shortest man.'

The Indian troops moved into Pakistan and launched a major offensive in the Lahore and Sialkot sectors. The troops reached the outskirts of Lahore. Strategically, this initiative was important to relieve the pressure on the Indian troops in the other sectors. Shastri is reported to have told General Chaudhuri, 'I want to reach Lahore before they enter Kashmir.' Today, many regard this initiative of Shastri as the first surgical strike. Once the hostilities ended, this act of Shastri made him a hero in the eyes of the people.

Years later, General Chaudhuri confided to Kuldip Nayar that by entering Pakistan, India wanted to destroy Pakistan's armoury and not to occupy its territory.[121] Years after the 1965 war, Air Force Chief Arjan Singh stated that there could not have been a better PM than Shastri to lead the country during the 1965 war. In the foreword to a book on Shastri, Singh writes that 1965 was the real test of his leadership and 'he passed with flying colours.'[122]

Anil Shastri, the son of Lal Bahadur Shastri, recalls the period prior to and after the war with Pakistan.[123] During that time, in cinema theatres, prior to the start of the screening of the movie, a news documentary used to be shown. Anil recalls that when Shastri appeared in these documentaries, people invariably compared him with Nehru. 'His short stature was perhaps a matter of ridicule for the audience at that time.'

---

[120]The then commander of the Western Command.

[121]Nayar, K. (2012). *Beyond the Lines: An Autobiography*. Roli Books Private Limited, p. 187

[122]Shastri, S. (2011). *Lal Bahadur Shastri: Past Forward*, New Delhi: Konark

[123]Choudary, P. & Shastri, A. (2015). *Lal Bahadur Shastri: Lessons in Leadership*, Delhi: Wisdom Village Publications, pp. 141–2

After the start of hostilities with Pakistan and when India took the decision to take the confrontation into Pakistani soil, Shastri 'suddenly earned respect from every corner of the country... It was after a long time in India's history that the battle was fought on enemy soil' and this achievement was largely attributed to the leadership that 'Lal Bahadur Shastri provided at that time... The same audience would clap and applaud the moment they would see their PM on the screen.' When Anil mentioned this to his father, he said, 'Great battles are won only if one has the will to fight. People admire the brave and not the meek.'

STANDING UP TO INTERNATIONAL PRESSURE

The Indian action invited world attention and there was a flurry of diplomatic activity. In a letter addressed to several heads of state, Shastri clarified the Indian position and reiterated that India's actions were essentially to defend the integrity of its boundaries[124]:

> ...our armed forces had no option but to take action against the bases in West Punjab from which the entire range of operations first across the Ceasefire Line, then across the international boundary with Jammu and Kashmir and finally, across the international boundary between India and Pakistan were mounted and assisted...
> I only want to emphasise to you that our action is purely defensive in character. All we are concerned with is preserving the integrity of our boundaries with Pakistan.

In spite of the tremendous pressure India came under,

---

[124]The PM's letters to several heads of state on 7 September 1965. *The Times of India*. (1965, September 10). From microfilms at NML.

Shastri stood his ground and defended the country's actions. In his meeting with U Thant, who visited both India and Pakistan, Shastri made it clear that a ceasefire would only be acceptable to India if Pakistan would refrain from committing aggression—open or covert—against India. Shastri also rejected the demand made by Pakistan that they would accept a ceasefire if India agreed to hold a plebiscite in J&K.[125] Based on the reports from the army and air chiefs, Shastri was now convinced that the destruction of the offensive capacity of Pakistan had been achieved and India was ready for a ceasefire, subject to assurances from Pakistan for the same. Shastri also took the Parliament into confidence and it must be said to his credit that representatives of all political parties extended their support to the government for the steps it was taking and its broad policy on the emerging situation with Pakistan.

While dealing with the Pakistani aggression, Shastri had to budget into the strategy the possibility of China intervening in the crisis. China had made it clear that they saw India as an aggressor and was siding with Pakistan. The critical question was: Would they directly intervene in the conflict? Given the experience of 1962, this factor was not merely a matter of concern for Shastri but for the entire nation watching the developments. As the military operations with Pakistan continued, China escalated the tensions by sending a protest note to India on 'successive serious violations of China's territory and sovereignty by Indian troops.' India felt that this protest was more to assure the Pakistani government of Chinese support.

While assessing the situation, Shastri was convinced that

[125]Srivastava, C.P. (1995). *Lal Bahadur Shastri: A Life of Truth in Politics*, Delhi: Oxford, pp. 257–8

China would not take any provocative action unless they could produce to the world some credible information of the allegations they had made against India. Shastri decided to adopt a two-fold approach on the matter: firstly, to firmly deny the Chinese allegations without provoking them to action, and secondly, if China did decide to take action, to be ready with a response. At this stage, China protested to India about constructions made on the Tibet side of the Tibet–Sikkim border and demanded that they be demolished in three days, failing which India should be ready to face 'grave consequences'. Shastri clarified India's position in the Lok Sabha[126]:

> The Government of India…[is] absolutely convinced that the allegations contained in the Chinese note… are completely groundless… [We] have no objection to a joint inspection of those points on the Tibet-Sikkim border where Indian personnel are alleged to have set up military structures in Tibetan territory. The Government of India on their part are prepared to arrange such an inspection, as early as possible, at an appropriate official level, on a mutually convenient date… We hope that China would not take advantage of the present situation and attack India. The House may be rest assured that we are fully vigilant and that if we are attacked, we shall fight for our freedom and with grim determination.

In his address to the Parliament on 17 September 1965, Shastri made three important points:

- Firstly, there was no ground for the Chinese allegations.
- Secondly, India was willing to offer a joint inspection

---

[126] *The Indian Express.* (1965, September 18). From microfilms at NML.

of the areas where China alleges that India has set up military structures.

◆ Finally, India was prepared for any military action that China may contemplate.

China decided not to escalate the crisis and responded by saying that the 'offending structures' had already been demolished by 'retreating Indian' troops. The Chinese deciding to de-escalate their tensions with India was seen by many as a success of Shastri's strategy and diplomatic initiatives. Shastri showed rare proof of his sense of humour, when in a public rally, he jokingly said that there was no question of India demolishing any offending structures when none were built in the first place.

FIRE AND DETERMINATION

As the conflict with Pakistan continued, it was becoming increasingly clear that the Pakistanis had suffered huge reverses. Finally, Pakistan conceded to a ceasefire on 23 September 1965, which India accepted. Shastri briefed the Parliament about the ceasefire. Two speeches during the discussion merit attention. J.B. Kripalani felt that the ceasefire had been accepted in a hurry to 'placate world opinion.' He felt that this 'compromise' will 'land us again and again in difficulties.' He, of course, conceded that if 'we fix a new line, then we will again be in difficulties.' The other speech was by Vijaya Lakshmi Pandit, who complimented Shastri for his 'bold leadership' in this crisis. In fact, Shastri was complimented by the entire House for his handling of this major crisis.

In his address to the nation, informing them of the ceasefire, Shastri had a warning for Pakistan. Any future misadventure in Kashmir or any other part of the country would be met with determination and full force. While he said that the 'blackout has been lifted...let us not mistake it for the dawn of peace.' In a very direct way, he was asking the people of India to be on alert and not assume that the hostilities with Pakistan had ended.

The belligerence of the Pakistani leadership was on constant display even after the ceasefire of 23 September 1965. The language that Bhutto used at the UN was openly provocative. Pakistan continued to maintain that any meaningful ceasefire would only be when the Kashmir issue was settled. Shastri stated India's position in unequivocal terms when he declared at a public event in Delhi that 'Kashmir is an integral part of India. So it will remain.' Later at a rally in Jaipur, he went a step ahead and said that Pakistan is a victim of delusion if it felt it could take Kashmir.

Shastri also decided to take on the Western powers, who were counselling India to be patient but not chastising Pakistan for its bellicose attitude. At a public event on 10 October 1965, Shastri made it clear that 'if others choose not to see our point of view, we will not take it lying down. If the Big Powers fail to see India's point of view, we will have to modify our attitude and reshape our policies.' In an earlier criticism of the Big Powers, he had asked, '[Just] because we are a big country, should we part with a portion of our territory whenever we are pressed to do so?'

Commenting on his attitude and approach and how Pakistan had totally misread his capacity and capability, he said in a moment of reflection on 10 October 1965, 'I may not show it, but there is plenty of fire and determination in me. We have had many momentous decisions to take during the last few weeks and I am sure you will agree that they were the right ones.'[127] Shastri made his stand unambiguous and 'thought it proper to move towards Lahore instead of sending a protest note or going to the Security Council.'

Shastri's quiet determination, boundless patience, steadfast confidence and untiring efforts were the building blocks of a successful effort by India to rebuff Pakistan's designs on Kashmir. Many were critical of the decision to accept a ceasefire by India. some of the factors that may have contributed to Shastri's decision are:

- Firstly, the professional advice he got from the military could have influenced the decision.
- Secondly, it could well be that Pakistani's military defences had been sufficiently weakened by India's taking the battle into their territory and thus the objective had been achieved.
- Finally, Shastri was an apostle of peace and wanted to give 'peace' yet another chance.

The phase after the formal cessation of hostilities and the coming into force of the ceasefire continued to see tensions in India–Pakistan relations. Under Shastri's leadership, six important steps were taken by India to defend its interests and to make its stand on the issues connected with Pakistan amply clear—both to the Indian public and to the world media:

- The Indian forces were kept in readiness to deal with any incursions that Pakistan indulged in.
- A series of public meetings were addressed by Shastri and his colleagues across India to convey to the people of India the achievement of the government in the conflict with Pakistan and its preparedness to deal

---

[127]Transcript of speech made on All India Radio.

with any eventuality even as it sought peace in the region.

◆ Shastri ensured that the government used every opportunity available to counter the comments by Pakistani leaders (especially its foreign minister) at international forums.

◆ Special emissaries were sent to key foreign heads of state by Shastri to explain India's position and stand.

◆ Shastri kept open the line of communication with key leaders, especially Lyndon Baines Johnson, the president of the US, and Alexei Kosygin, chairman of the Council of Ministers of the USSR.

◆ Shastri visited the forward areas to get a first-hand view of the commendable achievements of the Indian armed forces.

TWIN PILLARS OF INDIA'S NATIONHOOD

It was during this period that Shastri addressed the nation in a radio broadcast on 10 October 1965. This speech became historic, as it saw the coining of a phrase that Shastri has been synonymous with: *'Jai Jawan, Jai Kisan'*. This slogan became a symbol of the twin pillars of India's nationhood. On the agricultural front, he appealed to the farmers to increase their produce, the traders to be fair in marketing the produce at just rates and the consumers to exercise restraint while consuming the produce. Self-sufficiency in foodgrains needed to be a national goal. At the same time, the country needed to develop a defence framework that could protect the national interests and sovereignty of the land. Central to this process was the Indian soldier. It was to boost the people's self-confidence and protect the nation's self-interest that Shastri coined the slogan, which gained immediate popularity and captured the essence of India.

Even when the hostilities with Pakistan were at their peak, Kosygin had attempted to broker peace between Pakistan and India. The efforts of Kosygin had the support of both the US president and the British PM, as the three collectively felt that any effort to de-escalate tensions in the South Asia region would be in the larger interest of world peace. The only country slightly apprehensive of the Soviet initiative was China, and they had given expression to the same on quite a few occasions. Soon after the ceasefire came into force between India and Pakistan, Shastri made a statement in the Parliament on 23 September 1965, highlighting the initiative taken by the Soviet leadership[128]:

> I should like to inform the House that on 18 September 1965, I received a message from Mr Kosygin, Chairman of the Council of Ministers of the USSR, offering his good offices for bringing about improved relations between India and Pakistan. No one can ever contest the view that ultimately India and Pakistan will have to live together as peaceful neighbours. We cannot, therefore, say no to any efforts which may help to bring about such a situation, made by those who are sincere and genuine in their feelings of goodwill and friendship. I have, therefore, informed Mr Kosygin today that we would welcome his efforts and good offices.

---

[128] *The Times of India*. 14 September 1965.

PREPARING FOR TASHKENT

After detailed consultations, India agreed to participate in a summit meeting with Pakistan involving the leadership of the two countries to be held in Tashkent on the invitation of the Soviet leadership in January 1966. Shastri undertook thorough consultations and preparation for the summit. The discussions involved the key officers of the armed forces, diplomats and senior civil servants. Shastri held detailed meetings with his Cabinet colleagues, senior Congress leaders and the CMs of states. The leaders of the Opposition parties were also involved in the parleys. Ever since he had taken over as PM, Shastri had made the process of detailed consultation an integral part of his approach to problem-solving and decision-making.

Given his inexhaustible patience and unbounded energy, Shastri spent long hours going into minute details in preparation for the Tashkent summit. It was clear that at the summit, a few issues would come up for discussion. Firstly, the UN Security Council (UNSC) resolution calling for a withdrawal of armed personnel to positions held by them prior to 5 August 1965 would very much be on the table. Consequently, the acceding to the vacation of the Haji Pir Pass[129] would be an important point of negotiation. Shastri was keen on a 'no war' agreement and Pakistan's response to the same would be crucial. Finally, the Pakistani insistence on including Kashmir in any negotiation would be a major sticking point. The strategy to be adopted on all these issues was discussed at considerable length.

---

[129]The Haji Pir Pass is an important pass that connects Poonch to Uri in J&K. Haji Pir was captured by the Indian army during the 1965 war. This capture dealt a blow to the Pakistani army's plans of assaulting Uri and subsequently the Kashmir valley. A return to the 5 August 1965 position would involve the return of control over this pass to Pakistan.

On the eve of his departure for Tashkent, Shastri spoke of the need for ending armed hostilities between India and Pakistan and hoped that Pakistan would agree that 'our armies would not bear arms against one another.'[130] Both India and Pakistan and the host, Soviet Union, had different expectations from the Tashkent talks. The Soviet Union hoped that primacy would be accorded to implementing the UNSC resolution 211 of 20 September 1965[131] and resolution 214 of 27 September 1965[132]. India was keen on peace and a commitment from Pakistan for a no-war pact. Pakistan was keen that Kashmir be the central point of discussion.

DISCUSSIONS AT MULTIPLE LEVELS

The Indian and Pakistani delegations arrived in Tashkent on 3 January 1965 and the talks went on for a week. The discussions were at multiple levels. There were one-to-one meetings between PM Shastri and President Ayub Khan of Pakistan, between Soviet leader Kosygin and Shastri, and between Kosygin and Khan. There were delegation-level meetings between India and Pakistan as well as the meeting of the foreign ministers of India, Pakistan and the USSR. There was also an opening summit meeting and a concluding meeting involving the leaders of all the three countries.

Shastri had built up an excellent rapport with Kosygin during past meetings and this came handy during the intricate

---

[130]*Hindustan Times*. (1966, January 3). From microfilms at NML.

[131]That the ceasefire should take effect from Wednesday, 22 September 1965.

[132]After expressing concern that the ceasefire called for in resolutions 209, 210 and 211 (and agreed to by India and Pakistan) was not holding, the UNSC demanded that the parties honour their commitment and withdraw all armed personnel.

negotiations to arrive at an agreement at Tashkent. Shastri's dialogue with Khan was largely in Hindustani and Urdu. Shastri had learnt Urdu as a school student and was well versed in it. The discussions were cordial even when the two leaders had serious differences on issues. It became increasingly clear to both India and the Soviet Union that it would be easier to deal with Khan than to deal with his foreign minister, Bhutto. Shastri felt that Khan was 'practical', but Bhutto was someone who could 'throw the spanner in the works of India-Pakistani relations'.[133] Throughout the negotiations, Shastri ensured that he took his entire team into confidence. At each stage of the negotiation, he briefed the foreign and defence ministers, who had accompanied him along with other senior officers. The consensus model that appeared to be second nature to Shastri was clearly on display in the way he discussed issues with the Indian delegation.

As the negotiations proceeded, Kosygin would often travel back and forth between Shastri and Khan in order to arrive at an agreement. The major points of disagreement in the discussions were threefold:

- Adhering to the UNSC resolutions on the India–Pakistan conflict, which would require a retreat to the 5 August 1965 positions in terms of possession of territories.
- An agreement on a no-war pact that India was keen on.
- A reference to the Kashmir issue, which was a key demand of Pakistan.

On the retreat to the 5 August 1965 position, Shastri had

[133]Srivastava, C.P. (1995). *Lal Bahadur Shastri: A Life of Truth in Politics*, Delhi: Oxford. p. 379

detailed discussions with his Cabinet colleagues, Indian diplomats, senior civil servants and army commanders. While the Haji Pir Pass, which India had taken possession of during the conflict, was strategically significant, it was also conceded that in the larger interests of peace in the region, the same could be returned to Pakistan in order to go back to the 5 August 1965 position. Having secured a consensus on the matter, Shastri did inform Kosygin that 'in the interests of peace...[he] would accept the reciprocal return of all armed personnel to the position prior to 5 August 1965, which in effect means a return to the 1949 [ceasefire] line.' Kosygin immediately responded, saying that by 'this bold and wise decision...you have made a decisive contribution to securing peace and have greatly enhanced the prospects of success at Tashkent.'[134]

As there was no agreement between India and Pakistan on a no-war pact, Kosygin suggested to Shastri whether 'a reaffirmation by both sides of their obligation under the UN charter to use peaceful means only to settle disputes, without any recourse to the use of force' would be acceptable.[135] Shastri conceded to the point and it was now left to Kosygin to secure Khan's approval on the issue.

On the issue of Kashmir, Shastri was determined to stand firm, even if it were to result in no agreement at Tashkent. The maximum concession that Shastri gave was the agreement on a reference to Kashmir in the declaration, qualified and circumscribed by a clear and categorical reference to the Indian stand. Shastri, in a tone of unusual firmness, did mention to Kosygin that he would resign as PM rather than

[134]Srivastava, C.P. (1995). *Lal Bahadur Shastri: A Life of Truth in Politics,* Delhi: Oxford. p. 363
[135]Ibid.

compromise on India's sovereignty over Kashmir, which was non-negotiable. Kosygin reassured Shastri that he would never ask him 'to do anything which...is against the interests of India.'[136] Shastri also made clear that he would not postpone his departure from Tashkent, which was scheduled for the morning of 11 January, even if no agreement could be reached.

Shastri, in a conversation with his senior officers, was convinced that Khan wanted peace, but Bhutto was against an agreement. Shastri felt that Bhutto was 'smarting with rage because of the failure of his grand design on Kashmir.'[137] On the other hand, Shastri felt that Khan 'understands the ground realities and very possibly will opt for peace.' Close to the midnight of 9 January 1965, Shastri was proved right. Kosygin came to Shastri after meeting with Khan and told him, 'I have some good news. I have persuaded President Ayub to accept your text on Kashmir and on the reaffirmation of the obligation under the UN Charter not to use force in the settlement of disputes.'

TASHKENT AGREEMENT: SHASTRI RETURNS TO HIS INNERMOST GANDHIAN SELF

This paved the way for the signing of the historic Tashkent agreement on 10 January 1965. Throughout the negotiations at Tashkent, Shastri had been insisting on the no-war clause, but Khan remained elusive on the question and ultimately agreed to the obligations under the UN Charter eschewing the use of force. Khan and Shastri had developed a level of comfort in dealing with each other, and in the draft agreement, Shastri

---

[136]Srivastava, C.P. (1995). *Lal Bahadur Shastri: A Life of Truth in Politics*, Delhi: Oxford. p. 376
[137]Ibid., p. 379

was able to convince and persuade him to write the words 'without resort to arms' in his own handwriting. Bhutto made a big issue of this undertaking later, though Khan realized that if he returned home without an agreement, he would find it difficult to face the public.

Shastri was a bit concerned about the reaction back home in India, especially on India's agreeing to withdraw from the Haji Pir Pass. Shastri had spent considerable amount of time with senior Indian journalists who had accompanied him to Tashkent, explaining the rationale of India's decision in the larger interests of peace in the region. Shastri was convinced that withdrawal from the Haji Pir Pass was vital to the larger negotiations and the signing of the peace agreement. The reaction to the agreement back home was mixed, but generally favourable, involving an understanding of the Indian compulsions. While the Congress, Communist Party of India and Swatantra Party defended the Tashkent Agreement, the Jana Sangh and the PSP were critical of it as representing an 'unseemly compromise and unjustifiable accommodation.'[138]

Highlighting why he agreed to the provisions of the Tashkent Agreement, Shastri said in a breakfast conversation with L.P. Singh on the morning of the signing of the agreement[139]:

> Shastri said that he had chosen to seek peaceful and friendly relations with Pakistan in order to keep faith with the most precious legacy that the country had had from Mahatma Gandhi. If relations between India and Pakistan remained strained, holding the potential of another armed conflict, India would take the path

[138] *The Times of India.* 11 January 1966.

[139] Singh, L.P. (1996). *Portrait of Lal Bahadur Shastri: A Quintessential Gandhian.* Ravi Dayal Publisher, pp. 157–8

of military glory, and our unique heritage, the ideals of non-violence, truth and human brotherhood bequeathed to us by Gandhiji would be lost. Peace and good relations with Pakistan, he said, were essential if India was to preserve her soul, and that, he said, was the main reason why he had made the Tashkent Agreement... Shastri had returned to his innermost Gandhian self with all his heart.

UNIQUE BRAND OF POLITICAL LEADERSHIP

With the passing away of Nehru, Shastri had been called upon to lead the country. He had emerged as a consensus candidate in the Congress party largely on account of his acceptability to both the key leaders in the Congress—both at the national and state levels, as well as among the members of the CPP. Shastri enjoyed this wide support and endorsement on account of his leadership style and skill sets. His low-profile nature, the simplicity he displayed, the trust he evoked, his capacity to bring people together and resolve differences and, above all, his democratic approach to decision-making were his major strengths. In important ways, he represented a crucial departure from the style and approach of the past leadership (Nehru). This was his true strength, which increasingly became apparent as he established his presence as PM.

During his short tenure, he faced many a crisis and emerged stronger in each case. The consultative approach, which was the key element in his decision-making, was an important factor that contributed to his success. Having succeeded Nehru, who had led the country for seventeen years, there were often unfair comparisons that were made. Shastri's strength lay in his continuing the framework established by his predecessor even as he attempted crucial departures from the past in consonance with his approach and priorities. Shastri treaded a path and adopted an approach that was distinctly different from the past. His stature grew with every passing day. The manner in which he dealt with the food crisis, placed a premium on self-sufficiency and self-reliance, and defended the country in the light of the aggression from Pakistan, all bear testimony to the success of his approach to problem-solving and leadership.

Shastri also disarmed his critics, who saw him as only remaining in the shadow of his mentors or felt that he was not capable of being decisive. Without significantly deviating from the path of the past, he initiated a course correction that had a clear stamp of his unique way of doing things. The focus on agriculture, the consensus model of decision-making, the increased involvement of the party leaders in the consultative process, the taking of the Parliament and especially the leaders of the Opposition into confidence, the diplomatic success in dealing with neighbours like China and big powers like the US, the USSR and the UK and, above all, the strategy of taking the battle with Pakistan into its very own territories—the original 'surgical strike', are all categorical acknowledgements of choosing to tread a path that was distinctly different and unique to his very own mode of political leadership.

6

ASSESSING HIS LEGACY

The Tashkent Agreement was a major achievement of Lal Bahadur Shastri as the PM. His commitment to ensuring peace was reflected in the negotiations he held with Pakistani and Soviet leaders and in the ultimate signing of this agreement. Shastri was aware that he would have to face some hostile reactions back home to the agreement, but firmly held the view that on his return he could persuade the skeptics of the utility of the accord. This was, however, not to be, as Shastri passed away a few hours after having signed the agreement.

There are several accounts by individuals who accompanied Shastri on his trip to Tashkent describing the events around his death. Soon after his body was brought back to India, controversies emerged on whether it was a natural death. Questions were raised on the body turning blue, the presence of incision marks on it and the non-conduct of a post-mortem. Even to this day, the debate continues. Shastri's wife Lalita Devi had demanded an investigation into the circumstances of his death, suspecting foul play. While the Raj Narain Commission was appointed, its report has never been put out in the public domain. Requests made under the Right to Information Act, to disclose details relating to the investigations into Shastri's death have also been withheld in 'public interest'.

This narration would not focus on the controversies surrounding his passing away. However, a comparison among three important accounts of the developments of that day, culminating in Shastri's death, indicates several inconsistencies. Shastri's Secretary, C.P. Srivastava, makes a detailed recording of the events in his biography of Shastri.[140] Kuldip Nayar, who was Shastri's press secretary, in his autobiography, *Beyond the Lines*, makes references to Shastri's death and the events surrounding it. Finally, Home Secretary L.P. Singh, who was also present at Tashkent, speaks about these events in his book, *Portrait of Lal Bahadur Shastri*. There are several points on which the three accounts concur, but there are important areas of difference too.

All the three narrations speak of Shastri being fine on the evening of 10 January 1966, after the signing of the Tashkent Agreement and the dinner banquet hosted by the Premier, Kosygin. Shastri retired to his room and continued to be in discussion with his close aides, essentially monitoring responses back home to the agreement. As they were to fly to Kabul the next morning at 7 a.m., Shastri's aides retired to their rooms close to midnight. At around 1.20 a.m., Shastri appeared at the door of the room of his aides and asked for his personal doctor. He was escorted back to his room and the doctor soon arrived. On his way back to his room, Shastri was coughing incessantly and was asked to lie down on his bed. He drank some water and then lapsed into an unconscious state, never to recover again. While his personal physician tried to revive him and additional medical help was immediately rushed to his room, they were unable to resuscitate him.

---

[140]Srivastava, C.P. (1995). *Lal Bahadur Shastri: A Life of Truth in Politics*, Delhi: Oxford

Shastri had suffered two heart attacks earlier. The first was in 1959 when he was the HM of UP and the second was in June 1964 soon after he was sworn in as PM. The cardiologist who attended on Shastri had warned that a third attack could be fatal and requested Shastri to take certain precautions after the second one. Shastri preferred to focus on his work and responsibilities, as he felt that that was his primary duty, which he could not ignore. His health was not a major priority for him. Thus, when he had the third heart attack, those around, who knew his medical history, were aware that it could well be fatal.

UNANSWERED QUESTIONS

All the three accounts seem similar in terms of their narration. So, where then is the point of departure?

The differences appear to emerge in terms of the factors that caused the stress and strain leading to the third heart attack. Srivastava, who was with Shastri throughout the day on 10 January, records that the latter was cheerful and showed no signs of fatigue, mental or physical stress or unease. He concedes that Shastri was 'private and reticent' about his health and rarely spoke to anyone about it. Srivastava accompanied Shastri back to his room at the end of the reception hosted by the Soviet premier. After a brief conversation, Srivastava took his leave, as he had another meeting to attend. On his return from the meetings, when he was about to retire for the day, he was informed of Shastri's critical condition by his aides and rushed to Shastri's room. By the time he reached, Shastri had already breathed his last.

When Srivastava later had a conversation with those who were around Shastri during the last few hours, they reported that he was keen to know of the reactions back home to the agreement. He was told that the response was favourable, save for the two Opposition parties—the PSP and the Jana Sangh. Shastri responded by saying, 'They are in the Opposition and it is their right to be critical.' Shastri wanted to speak to his family members, but his wife could not hear him clearly and so he spoke to his younger son-in-law and a few other family members. His son-in-law assured him that the reaction in India was good and people hailed his success at Tashkent.

L.P. Singh records that at Tashkent, Shastri showed no signs of physical unease or fatigue. He wondered whether Shastri's 'courtesy, patience and equanimity were not bought at the tremendous nervous cost and resulted in the corrosion of his health.' Singh believes that the rough and tumble that accompanied the brief period when he led the country, could not 'but undermine his not very robust physical constitution.' Singh is convinced that Shastri died of a sudden, severe heart attack. Singh also met medical experts who told him that Shastri had the best medical support that was possible at Tashkent.

Kuldip Nayar's narration varies marginally. Nayar says that soon after signing the Tashkent Agreement, there was some anxiety in Shastri about the responses back home to the agreement. On returning to his room after attending Kosygin's reception, Shastri spoke to his personal assistants back home in India on the reactions to the agreement. He was told that there was general support but at Shastri's own home, there was some unhappiness. When Shastri spoke to some family members, they expressed their reservations about the agreement. When Shastri was told that his wife also did not approve of the agreement, Nayar reports that Shastri said, '*Agar gharwalon ko accha nahin laga, to baharwale kya kahenge?*' (If people in the family did not like it, what will outsiders say?). Shastri then paced up and down in his room. Nayar believes that the 'telephone conversations, the journalists' attitude, and the walk must have been a strain that night.'

Here, two points merit attention:

- *First, the charge that Shastri's body had turned blue by the time it arrived in India*: This, it is believed, was on account of a chemical injection administered to his body to avoid rapid decomposition. The embalming liquid was injected through an incision into the femoral artery, which also explains the marks on the body.

- *Secondly, why was there no post-mortem done?*: L.P. Singh explains that the Soviets had mentioned that it was a procedure to conduct the post-mortem examination of the body of a high functionary.[141] Singh goes on to add that as home secretary, he had advised against it as the 'post mortem was...considered something bordering on defilement of a dead body.' In the light of Shastri's medical history of heart attacks, the death seemed natural and a post-mortem was uncalled for.

The debate continues to rage and resurface at a regular frequency.

THE FINAL JOURNEY

On receiving the news of Shastri's health condition, the entire Indian delegation had gathered around his room. Premier Kosygin and other Soviet leaders soon arrived as did the

---

[141]Singh, L.P. (1996). *Portrait of Lal Bahadur Shastri: A Quintessential Gandhian*. Ravi Dayal Publisher, p. 162

Pakistani President, Ayub Khan. On seeing Shastri's mortal remains, Khan said, 'Here is a man of peace, who gave his life for amity between India and Pakistan... [We] might have solved...differences had he lived.'[142]

Arrangements were soon made to fly the mortal remains of Shastri to India. The Soviets arranged for an aircraft to fly Shastri's body along with the rest of the Indian delegation. When the cortège carrying Shastri's body (that had been placed in a casket) reached the airport, Ayub Khan was waiting among others to receive it. When the casket was lowered from the gun carriage, Kosygin and Khan were the main pallbearers carrying the coffin on their shoulders towards the waiting aircraft. One would find it difficult to find another example in history of the leader of a nation that had consistently adopted an attitude of belligerency with another nation till the signing of a peace agreement, carry the mortal remains of the leader of the nation it considered its rival. To a certain extent, this was also testimony to the admiration and respect that Shastri evoked.

Shastri's mortal remains were received by a grieving nation, which was still to recover from the shock of losing its PM. His body was kept for people to pay their homage. Common people from all walks of life filed past his body and paid their firal respects. Political leaders from within India and representing foreign nations also came to pay their final tributes. Shastri was cremated on 12 January 1966 with full state honours at Vijay Ghat, which was adjacent to both Raj Ghat (where Gandhiji was cremated) and Shanti Van (where Nehru's cremation was done). Shastri's final rites took place

---

[142]Nayar, K. (2012). *Beyond the Lines: An Autobiography*. Roli Books Private Limited, pp. 201–2

next to the memorials of two people who greatly influenced his politics and shaped his career. *The Washington Post* correspondent Warren Unna reported on 13 January 1966: 'Mankind historically has reserved its greatest occasions for the final journeys of its leaders—and India today made such an occasion.'[143]

A PARENTHESIS IN HISTORY?

Lal Bahadur Shastri departed from the scene much before the country could truly benefit from his full potential. During his nineteen months as PM, one got many glimpses of his unique style of leadership. Much of these months were spent in settling down and dealing with one crisis after another. It was truly in the last few months, when the hostilities with Pakistan reached its peak and Shastri demonstrated the courage of conviction to launch an offensive against Pakistan to fight back its belligerency, that the nation finally sat up to acknowledge the power of his leadership. Yet, he left, just as the nation was becoming truly aware of his true capacities.

The Tashkent declaration could well have been a turning point. As Ayub Khan himself conceded, if Shastri had lived, the prospects for establishing lasting peace between the two countries would have been much brighter. Even as Shastri prepared for the Tashkent meetings, he saw a moment to bring peace and stability to the region. On the morning of the signing of the Tashkent Agreement, he did confide to his advisers that the accord he was due to sign would help India preserve her soul as a votary of peace and strengthen its commitment to the ideals of Gandhi. His earnest appeal to the

---

[143]From microfilms at NML.

journalists from India, who accompanied him to Tashkent, was to reflect on the positives of the accord, rather than exclusively focusing on the negatives. Any negotiation, he felt, involved a give and take and he was convinced, that the gains that India would achieve from this agreement far outweighed what was being conceded. Shastri was determined to return to India after the agreement and go around convincing people as well as political leaders that the agreement he had signed was in the best interests of India and for durable peace in the region. Fate, however, willed otherwise.

How does one assess the legacy of Shastri? Some would assert that his short tenure as PM left limited scope for him to leave a lasting impact. His ministerial colleague T.T. Krishnamachari remarked that Shastri could well be a 'parenthesis in history.'[144] More critically, given the focus of the Congress party on the leadership of the Nehru-Gandhi family, PMs from within the Congress, who hailed from outside this framework, have not received the spotlight they truly deserved. Shastri's prime ministership was sandwiched between that of a father and daughter—Jawaharlal Nehru and Indira Gandhi— both of whom had reasonably long tenures as PMs. If Nehru was the PM for an uninterrupted term of seventeen years, Gandhi was in power, in two phases, for over fifteen years. In comparison, Shastri led the country for a mere nineteen months. History often remembers leaders not so much for their contributions during a short period of time but for the impact of their sustained and long-term presence. Added to this is the fact that the Congress party has, over time, focused rather exclusively, on the contribution of its leaders who hailed

---

[144]Nayar, K. (2012). *Beyond the Lines: An Autobiography*. Roli Books Private Limited, p. 203

from the Nehru-Gandhi family. This has clearly resulted in Shastri not being accorded the stature and position he rightly and richly deserves.

MULTILAYERED CONTRIBUTIONS

As I researched for this book, the multilayered contributions of Shastri came to the fore. Weaving together the different anecdotes and snippets of information led me to understand both the complexity of the challenges he faced as well as the simplicity of the approach he adopted. If one were to assess his life and times from the days he entered the freedom movement to the time he led the country as PM, five vital strands of this legacy evidently stand out. As a wrap-up of this summary, an attempt is made to catalogue these aspects of Shastri's legacy, of course, in a random order.

A People's Person

Shastri would be remembered as a people's person who dealt with all individuals with trust, tact and transparency. The trust quotient that Shastri evoked was extremely high. One would not come across examples of his letting down a colleague. His mentors reposed implicit faith in him as did his peers and followers. This was on display at all those moments when he was given organizational responsibilities in the Congress party, be it at the district level in Allahabad, at the state level in UP, or finally at the national level. Trust was a crucial factor that helped him resolve ticklish problems and made him the most sought-after negotiator, who Nehru implicitly depended upon. Shastri was also known for his tact in dealing with people and their problems. This explains why he had no enemies. He often disarmed his critics with the sincerity of his intentions. Shastri had that very positive approach even when disagreeing with someone's perspective. He had this special skill of saying no in an acceptable and dignified way, which left the other party with little choice but to accept Shastri's standpoint with grace and humility. One wonders if Morarji would have so easily conceded the leadership race in 1964 if Shastri was not the one he was pitted against. Much earlier, both in 1952 and in 1957, when he played a key role in choosing the candidates for the Congress party to contest the Lok Sabha and Assembly elections, it was this tact that saw him resolve messy squabbles and intense factional feuds. This trust and tact were accompanied by yet another virtue—his transparent approach. There was no mask that Shastri wore. He said what he felt and did what he said. Yet, he said it with such simplicity and humility that it was rarely perceived as offensive or causing any hurt. This transparency of approach was towards all those he had a chance to meet and interact with, be it his family members and relations, his officers and advisers, fellow politicians, associates and party workers or the common citizen. This openness that Shastri demonstrated won the admiration and respect of Premier Kosygin during the Tashkent negotiations. The same transparency was evident when he managed to work out a solution to settle the dispute relating to the authenticity of the relic preserved at the Hazratbal shrine. This transparent approach was also what convinced C. Subramaniam to accept the food and agriculture portfolio when Shastri constituted his Cabinet.

Cooperation, Consensus and Consultation

Shastri's second legacy was a leadership style that was rooted in cooperation, consensus and consultation. In any position he held, Shastri sought the cooperation of all those involved in the organizational or decision-making process. Bureaucrats who worked with him were all praise for his approach to arriving at a decision that involved respecting the views of people and encouraging them to fearlessly make their point. Shastri had the skill to listen to diverse viewpoints, weigh the possible options and then arrive at a decision. In all the challenges he was asked to resolve by PM Nehru, the first step Shastri initiated was enlisting the cooperation of all those who were part of the dispute. He made every segment feel comfortable, respected and gave them a patient hearing. This by itself resolved much of the crisis. As PM, he sought the cooperation and support of the Opposition leaders and briefed them about major policy initiatives. Within the party, he consulted senior leaders and took the CWC into confidence. While some saw this approach of extensive consultation as a sign of weakness and inability to take swift decisions, Shastri himself was quite firm in endorsing the strengths of this approach. He was of the firm view that if the process of consultation to negotiate a consensus solution was time-consuming, it also led to a decision that was much more broad-based in terms of support. He went on to add that there were several occasions when, if the circumstances so warranted, a swift decision was often made without compromising on the consultative mechanisms in place. One noticed this at the time of both dealing with the food crisis as also during the Pakistani intrusion into India. Though his own party members had charged Shastri with being a 'prisoner of indecision', they were later quick to appreciate the speed and firmness with which he responded to Pakistan and its adventurism on the borders.

Through his skills of negotiation, Shastri was able to create a win-win situation, with each party happy to acknowledge the tangible takeaways from the negotiating table. While resolving the language crisis in Assam or the anti-Hindi agitation on the question of the official language of the Union or even while restoring the balance and harmony in India–Nepal relations, he was able to arrive at a negotiated settlement that left each segment feeling that they emerged from the crisis with an element of respectability, fair play and justice. His patience and energy played a key role in ensuring that all parties to a conflict felt that they were being treated with honour and dignity and given a patient hearing.

Leadership style is invariably linked to the personality of the said leader. A gross injustice that we do to leaders is comparing them to their predecessors and judging and evaluating them in the context of the past. Shastri had neither the flamboyance nor the charisma of Nehru. He was assertive in an understated way and got his way with people with persuasion and reasoning. Thus, for Shastri, the context defined the content of his style. Initially, when the memories of Nehru were still fresh, there were inevitable comparisons that people made between Shastri and Nehru. However, gradually, people saw Shastri not from the prism of Nehru, but from the unique space that Shastri independently created. Especially, towards the end of his term, Shastri had clearly emerged as a leader with his own distinct style and approach to decision-making.

Ensuring Equality

A third legacy for which Shastri will always be remembered was his unwavering commitment to ensuring equality, fighting against all forms of injustice and waging a war against corruption. This commitment was seen not merely in what he said but in his actions too. Shastri was known to treat all those who came to meet him with courtesy and respect. Everyone was given a patient hearing and no one left without being able to voice their concerns. As a minister in the government, Shastri did not seek any special privileges and insisted on not taking any step that would inconvenience the common people. He would often side-step protocol and move among people like an ordinary citizen. His aides recall that once as Union HM, his vehicle was held up at a railway crossing. He got down and asked his aides to accompany him to a sugar cane juice vendor on the roadside. After everyone had enjoyed the juice, he insisted on paying for it and then returned to the car to continue his journey. His simplicity and humility led to the sugar cane vendor not realizing that he had served the Union HM, who had even paid up for the juice consumed by his team. This is, of course, unimaginable in present times.

Having grown up in poverty and hardship, Shastri understood the challenges that the common people faced. During his days in the SPS, he worked with the socially and economically marginalized and understood the hierarchical nature of Indian society. He was committed to addressing this socio-economic injustice and used every opportunity while in power to address the same. He sought to sensitize the police to people's problems as the HM of UP. Law and order for him was not merely about enforcing the authority of the government but of understanding the challenges of the people. As railway minister at the centre, he focused attention on improving the conditions and facilities for passengers travelling in the third class. He ultimately convinced his department to create only two classes in the railways. As industry and commerce minister, he focused attention on the agro and rural industries. As the PM, he drew the attention of the Planning Commission to agriculture. He felt that the food crisis was on account of the consistent neglect of this sector in the years after Independence. Shastri raised objections when friends and associates indulged in caste discrimination. On several occasions he refused to partake of meals at functions if those belonging to the Dalit community were discriminated against. His sense of gender justice was evident in his decision soon after Independence, as the transport minister of UP, to introduce female bus conductors in government buses. His many speeches as PM made frequent references to the fight against social injustices and the need to end caste-based discrimination.

Whenever the occasion required, Shastri also took a principled stand against corruption. As HM of the Union, he brought to PM Nehru's attention the report of the investigation against Union Minister K.D. Malaviya, who was found guilty of corruption. Nehru immediately thought it fit to seek the resignation of Malaviya, which, to a certain extent, soured the relationship between Malaviya and Shastri. He was instrumental in the appointment of the Santhanam Committee to suggest ways and means of dealing with corruption. The committee submitted its report when Shastri was PM and he got the key recommendations implemented. During his prime ministership, several senior ministers at the Union and state level resigned on accounts of allegations of corruption. Punjab CM P.S. Kairon was required to quit when a Supreme Court judge held him guilty of corruption. Orissa CMs Biren Mitra and Biju Patnaik faced prosecution on account of their being held guilty of the same charges by another Supreme Court judge. Finance Minister Krishnamachari thought it fit to resign when Shastri favoured an investigation by the Chief Justice of India on a chargesheet that had been filed against the finance minister. It was clear that Shastri would take a firm stand against corruption, especially when it involved those holding high offices. This was clearly non-negotiable for him.

An Apostle of Peace

Shastri will be remembered as an apostle of peace who remained strongly committed to the national interest. In his first address to the nation as PM, he reaffirmed his commitment to promoting peace with all countries of the world in general and India's neighbours in particular. He made it a point to stop over in Karachi on his way back from the Non-Aligned Summit at Cairo, to commence a dialogue with Pakistani leaders. Even after the incursions by the Pakistanis in the RoK, Shastri preferred to act with caution and not rush to any decision. Pakistan miscalculated Shastri's patience and poise as representing his unwillingness to challenge them. Yet, when Pakistan launched a major offensive in Kashmir, Shastri not only defended Indian territories but decided to take the battle into Pakistani soil. Even though he was a votary of peace, he was willing to strike back and use force if protecting India's national interest demanded it. While preparing for the Tashkent conference, Shastri had detailed discussions with the military commanders, his advisers and key members of the Cabinet on whether India should agree to withdraw from the Haji Pir Pass in the larger interests of peace and return to the pre-war situation. Only when he secured the support of these key set of people, did he decide to convey to Soviet Premier Kosygin that India would be willing to withdraw to the pre-war boundaries as long as Pakistan too adhered to that and in the larger interests of building peace in the region.

Shastri was anxious of the response among the Indian people, journalists and the political class on the provisions of the Tashkent Agreement. He was aware of the misgivings among some sections, but felt that he would be able to convince those critics of the rationale of the treaty to forge peace in the subcontinent.

The primacy that Shastri accorded to peaceful solutions was not merely in dealing with neighbours and other countries but was also evident in the problem-solving techniques he adopted to resolve domestic challenges. From the time he was the HM in UP, his approach to problems was from the prism of securing a peaceful solution that was acceptable to all. This was his guiding principle at all times. His experience of working on the ground while participating in the freedom struggle and as a member of the SPS convinced him that resolving socio-economic and political conflicts was about placing a premium on peaceful and non-violent techniques. In that sense, he was the true inheritor of the legacy of Mahatma Gandhi and sought to consciously and conscientiously tread the path championed by the Father of the Nation.

The fact that Shastri was respected even by those who opposed his political views is indicative of his unequivocal commitment to building bonds of commonality, rooted in a sense of fairness, understanding and reconciliation. At Tashkent, during the peace talks, he understood that Ayub Khan was keen to establish peace and take back an agreement to salvage his political position and reputation. He also knew that the biggest stumbling block on the Pakistani side was Foreign Minister Bhutto, who had an eye on his own political future. Shastri's negotiation skills led to his playing on his strengths and convincing Khan even as he neutralized the damage that Bhutto had the potential to cause.

In the larger interests of stability in the region and as a staunch believer in the Gandhian values of peace and non-violence, Shastri decided to give harmony and peaceful coexistence a chance. He felt that this was the way he could help the country preserve its soul. His passing away on the night of the signing the agreement denied him that opportunity to build on the agreement and take the peace process forward in the way he had envisioned.

Passionate and Compassionate

Finally, Shastri's most critical legacy is his statesmanship. He worked with passion, led with compassion and achieved with conviction. In whatever responsibility Shastri took on or was entrusted, he worked with a passion and zeal that was demonstrably evident. It gleamed in his eyes and showed in the sincerity of his words and determination of his actions. Unmindful of his frail health, he continued to maintain a punishing schedule. When people reminded him that he needed to take adequate rest, he would respond that his first commitment was to the task assigned to him and if it impacted his health, so be it.

The 'human touch' was visible in the way Shastri inspired people to follow his lead. Truly democratic in his orientation and style, as the PM, his Cabinet meetings saw detailed and frank discussions and the true practice of collective responsibility. His Cabinet colleagues were aware that he would back them to the hilt if their actions were in the larger public interest and did not compromise on any ethical principles. At the end of the day, Shastri was able to convince different stakeholders of the need to pursue a particular line of action. In each of the crises he resolved, he was able to convince all segments of society with the power of his conviction. His persuasive skills, rooted in his commitment to values, and his visible genuineness allowed him to take all sections of the society along.

◆

Shastri was truly a leader of the masses who emerged from the masses and understood the masses. Even when he reached the highest office of the land, he did not lose touch with the ground reality. His humility, simplicity and self-effacing nature were his greatest strengths, which never allowed him to lose touch with the actual world or get carried away by the artificiality that power often brought with it. Till the very end, he was always concerned about how the common people would view his actions. Viewing things from the vantage position of the Indian on the street was his constant endeavour. This truly made him a hero of the masses. He became an idol, not by the flamboyance of his style or the magnetism of his presence or even the charm of his words, but by rising to that status on account of the sincerity of his convictions, commitment to his principles and capacity to carry all sections of society on the path he walked.

ACKNOWLEDGEMENTS

Shastri always fascinated me and the more I read about him, the more I realized that he had not been accorded the importance and recognition that he deserved. He was a leader who rose from the grass roots and had the opportunity to work at the local, state and then national level. He represented, in important ways, the common Indian. Thus, when the opportunity came to delve deeper into Shastri's life, I made the best use of the opportunity. As I was researching, I came to admire his leadership style and approach to dealing with people. The refreshing contrast he represented was obvious.

I had the privilege of having very inspiring teachers. I would like to thank all of them for having instilled in me that thirst for learning and a spirit of inquiry. In the last thirty-seven years, I have had the chance to interact with more than 15,000 students. Each of them has allowed me to learn with them in the classroom. This has been one of the most enriching experiences and I am beholden to them for this opportunity.

I would like to thank Dr Chenraj Roychand, the president of the Jain Trust for having encouraged me to pursue my research interests and discussed this project in great detail. I must also acknowledge the benefit of and insights gained during the many discussions with Dr Suhas Palshikar, a close friend and associate for more than a quarter of a century. My colleagues at the Centre for Research in Social Sciences and Education at Jain University provided all the support to complete this work. I would like to acknowledge the support of my colleagues, Dr Priyanca Mathur Velath and Dr Mythili Rao, for having understood and supported my request for them to take on more responsibilities at the workplace to help me complete this work. I would like to thank Dr Kalpana Muralidharan for helping in data collection and analysis.

I wish to thank my wife Shailaja, who has been as excited as me about this project; and my son Sanjal, who enquired every day from Auckland about the progress on the book and kept up the enthusiasm levels. To all my friends and colleagues with whom I discussed this work as it was progressing—a very big thank you.

I would like to thank the Rupa team for their support and gentle persuasion to complete the tasks on time. And of course, I take full responsibility for the analysis and material outlined in this book. I do hope the readers enjoy what I have reflected on and would welcome their feedback.

Praise for the Book

Lal Bahadur Shastri, the unassuming, consensus-building prime minister, restored to us dignity and self-confidence, which we lost in the 1962 debacle. Dr Sandeep Shastri does well to remind us that though his tenure was only nineteen months, PM Shastri provided decisive leadership, and tried to clean up corruption in high places.

—Shakti Sinha, Director, Nehru Memorial Museum & Library, and former secretary to Prime Minister Atal Bihari Vajpayee

The life and times of Lal Bahadur Shastri are a less chronicled aspect of contemporary India. Truth is, Shastri was a politician of integrity and complexity whose legacy is trapped between that of Nehru and Indira. In this carefully researched book, Dr Sandeep Shastri draws on all his knowledge of politics and society to do great justice to one of the towering political figures of modern India, whose inspiring life is a reminder of just what true public service is really about.

—Rajdeep Sardesai, Consulting Editor, India Today television

Sandeep Shastri's biography of Lal Bahadur Shastri is filling an important gap in the literature as this figure of Indian politics has remained understudied for too long. While his tenure as prime minister has been very short, it has played a key part in the political trajectory of India, vis-à-vis Pakistan because of the 1965 war, but also domestically. Shastri's contribution shows that Congress could always rely on remarkable leaders out of the Nehru-Gandhi family.

—Christophe Jaffrelot, professor of South Asian politics and history, the Centre d'études et de recherches internationales (CERI) at Sciences Po, Paris

Lal Bahadur Shastri has invited us to think of a counter-factual: What would have been the course of political events, the Congress party and, indeed, Indian history, if he had not passed away so suddenly? This first academic study of the life and legacy of Shastriji brings out not just his famed personal virtues of simplicity and honesty but also his political skills of consultation, cooperation and consensus-building. Professor Sandeep Shastri combines deep empathy with rigorous scholarship to fill a major gap in the existing scholarship and lay the foundations for future research in political biographies.

—**Yogendra Yadav, president,**
Swaraj India party and leading political scientist

INDEX